EVERYTHING NEW DRIVERS NEED TO KNOW

How to Pass the Driving Test, Avoid Accidents, Handle Car Breakdowns, Decode Road Signs, and Become the Safest Driver on the Road!

Peter Myers

ISBN: 978-1-962496-06-3

For questions, please reach out to
Support@OakHarborPress.com

Please consider leaving a review!

Just visit: OakHarborPress.com/Reviews

FREE BONUS

GET OUR NEXT BOOK FOR FREE!

Scan or go to:

OakHarborPress.com/Free

TABLE OF CONTENTS

INTRODUCTION

Congratulations! You're either a new driver, about to become a new driver, or have a new driver in your family! Learning to drive is an exciting milestone that comes with a lot of anticipation and intimidation. Everyone who drives can remember the feelings of accomplishment when earning their driver's license. Learning to drive may seem like a daunting task, but the level of freedom it grants is worth the challenge!

When learning, there are many skills to master if you want to become a competent and safe driver. In this book, you will learn the basic process for receiving your license, tips for practicing driving safely, common road laws and rules, learning about your vehicle, and how to handle accidents. Although this book is designed to get you started, learning to drive is a life-long process that relies heavily on practice.

Each state has different requirements for earning your learner's permit and license. In this book, we will cover each state's basic requirements. After receiving your permit, it is highly recommended to take a driver's education course—some states even require it. These courses provide a safe environment for you to experience your first hours on the road and learn more about the road rules specific to your state. Your local DMV may have lists of certified instructors in your area available.

Getting behind the wheel is a big responsibility, and to be a good driver, you need to do a lot more than just pass the test. It is essential to practice and study to keep you, your family, and other drivers on the road safe. Remember, you are sharing the road with other drivers, each with a different level of experience, as well as motorcyclists, bicyclists, and pedestrians. You have little control over other people, but you can control yourself. Mindfulness and practice will help you learn how to react appropriately to the environment around you.

When you begin your driving practice sessions, don't try to rush into things too quickly. We all know driving is exciting, but don't start with a six-hour road trip. Start learning on less populated streets, in clear weather, and during the daytime. This will help you gain confidence in your abilities behind the wheel before you begin driving under different conditions. It is a good idea to plan your driving route and choose an area you are already familiar with before setting out. Knowing where the stop signs, lights, four-way stops, and turns are in advance will make your first driving experiences less stressful.

The practice sessions that you will do are precisely that: Practice! Once you have your permit, you will drive with someone who is already licensed. It is important to take advantage of this period while you have the expertise of a veteran driver riding with you. It is a good idea to drive during night, under various weather conditions, and in different areas. Driving in a city or on a freeway is much different than in a neighborhood or on back roads. Having the advice, guidance, and extra set of eyes with you while you explore these new areas can help tremendously with building confidence and knowledge. Sometimes it may seem frustrating, especially if the person riding with you seems stressed, but remember that the immediate feedback is helping you become a better driver and leading you towards a higher level of freedom.

There are a lot of accidents that happen because of distracted driving or even issues with the vehicle. While this is a common problem, it is avoidable with the proper precautions. Make sure to wear your seatbelt, obey traffic laws, and put your phone away. This is not only for your safety but for the safety of those around you. Things happen, whether you are running late, playing music, on your phone, or talking to your friends. All of these can be distractions from the road, and that is when things can go very wrong very quickly.

When you are driving, not only do you need to stay safe for yourself, but you also have people who love you and want you to be safe. It is essential to keep them in mind when you are tempted to be distracted or drive unsafe. Other people operate with the mindset of driving as if there was a cop around. The last thing anyone wants is to get pulled over or get into an accident, so keeping the mindset that a cop is right around the corner is an easy way to keep focused on what's right in front of you: the open road.

This book will answer many of your questions and help you learn about important elements in driving that you may not have thought about. This is just the beginning of your journey. You will continue to learn new skills throughout your life, and the first step is to learn the basics.

PRACTICE MAKES PERFECT!

No matter what you are pursuing, practice is necessary to become good and comfortable. You would not be able to jump onto a piano and immediately perform one of Beethoven's most complicated symphonies. You would have to learn the keys and how to play individual notes, growing into the ability to play that intricate symphony. Like the piano, driving a car is something that you should learn how to do gradually, increasing the difficulty of the driving scenarios as you practice more and build more confidence.

HOW TO PRACTICE DRIVING

Before getting into a vehicle, the first step is to learn about your vehicle. This includes learning how to turn on the headlights, use the windshield wipers, turn signals, and any other features you might need to utilize when driving. Although most vehicles are similar, different makes and models will position the buttons and levers in slightly different positions. You can find this information in the drivers manual or simply spend some time familiarizing yourself with the vehicle's functions.

These essential things are in similar places in the vehicle. When you are sitting in the driver's seat looking at the steering wheel, the turn signal is usually the lever on the left-hand side of the steering wheel. If you push the lever up, the right turn signal will turn on. If you push the lever down, the left turn signal will turn on. To turn off the turn signal, you will need to bring that lever back to the neutral center position.

To turn on the headlights, there are two common places that this will be. On the dashboard, on the left-hand side, there may be a dial that you need to turn to turn on your headlights. If the knob is not on the dashboard, it may be a turn dial on the end of the lever on the left-hand side of the steering wheel. Headlights are essential when it is dark outside or during dawn and dusk. You are also required to have your headlights turned on when your windshield wipers are on.

To turn on your windshield wipers, you would use the lever on the right-hand side of the steering wheel. Turning the dial will increase or decrease the speed of the windshield wiper blades, while moving the lever up and down will turn the wipers on and off.

The hazard lights are important in an emergency or in case you need to pull over on the shoulder of the road for any reason. This is usually a button marked by a triangle symbol. For some vehicles this is located above the steering wheel or on the dashboard. On other vehicles it is found near the radio controls. Hazard lights will cause all of your lights to flash simultaneously to alert other vehicles of your presence or sudden need to pull over.

The actions that you need to take while driving is simple to remember. The gas pedal makes the vehicle move, while the brake pedal causes the vehicle to stop, and the steering wheel is what you use to guide the car in the direction that you want to go. While the fundamentals are easy to remember, putting them into practice can be intimidating.

When looking at the pedals of a vehicle, you may see two or three pedals. The pedal on the far right is the gas pedal. This is typically the smaller pedal that you would use to accelerate the vehicle and maintain speed. To the left of the gas pedal is the brake, which generally is the largest of the pedals. This is the pedal that you will use to apply the brakes. If you apply light pressure to the brake pedal, this will slow the vehicle, and as you apply more pressure, the car will come to a stop. If you are driving a manual car, there will be a third pedal on the left side of the brake called the clutch.

It's also important to know how to do basic things like putting gas in the car, which type of fuel needs to be used when putting gas into your vehicle, checking your tire pressure, or even changing a tire. The worst thing that you can do is expect to learn these things as you go; this will only cause a lot of frustration when you are learning to drive.

After you complete your research about your vehicle, it is time to find someone to drive with. When you are practicing driving with your learner's permit, you need to have a licensed driver with you. Make sure that the person you are learning to drive with is a trusted, experienced licensed driver or even a professional driving instructor. The experience that they have is a valuable resource when learning how to drive.

Along with knowing the basics about the vehicle you will be driving and choosing the right driving instructor, it is crucial to do a pre-driving vehicle check to make sure that everything is running and operating correctly. This will help prevent things from happening to the vehicle while driving. In this pre-driving check, make sure to check the gas level and tire pressure and make sure that all of your lights are working correctly.

After making sure that the vehicle is in prime operating condition, it is important to adjust all of the mirrors to your specific needs. The mirrors will be one of the most used tools you will use when you are driving, and they will be used most often. To adjust your side view mirror, there is generally a joystick on the driver's side door that you would use to adjust the mirrors.

Make sure that when you adjust the mirrors, you are sitting in the driver's seat, with the seat positioned where you can easily access the gas pedal, the brake pedal, the gear shifter, and the steering wheel. Begin on the driver's side mirror, making sure that you can see the road behind you and a small piece of your vehicle. Next, you will adjust the mirror on the passenger side in the same way. You should see the road behind you on the passenger side and a small part of your vehicle. To adjust your rearview mirror, you should gently grab the mirror and move it so that you can see out of the back windshield without having to move your head.

After you have learned everything that you need to know about your vehicle and have the seat and mirrors adjusted, you are ready to begin practicing how to drive. Learning how to drive in a phased approach is important as you master basic skills before advancing to the next phase in the process.

During your introductory lessons, while you may feel like you are ready to just get onto the road, these lessons are what are going to be key in making sure that you can get behind the wheel successfully on the open road.

The basic skills that you will begin learning are the basics of operating a vehicle, such as turning on the car, changing gears, accelerating, braking, driving in reverse, or using the turn signal, which are all things that you need to feel comfortable with before getting onto the road.

When you feel comfortable with the basic functions associated with driving a car, it is finally time to get on to the road and put those skills into action. Getting on the road can be nerve-wracking with all the new things you need to pay attention to. The vehicles driving next to you can be intimidating and it's often an anxiety point for the first few times on the road. Just know that you are not alone. If you are feeling this type of anxiety, take a deep breath and keep going. It will be okay!

During the second phase of your driving practice, focus on putting your skills into practice in ideal real-life situations, meaning during the day when the weather is ideal, and road conditions are clear. This will allow you to concentrate on driving with traffic and signals you are not used to driving with at this point. Just like when you were learning the basics of driving, this phase may take a bit longer to adjust. If you are someone who takes longer to get comfortable in these driving situations, that is not a bad thing; you are a new driver and still learning.

An ideal time to begin this second phase of driving practice would be in the late morning or around lunchtime. It is also important to make sure that you are avoiding peak driving hours, like rush hour. The number of other vehicles and other obstacles during this kind of traffic can be overwhelming, even for seasoned drivers, let alone new drivers like you.

After you have mastered driving on the road in ideal conditions, this is when you can begin to learn how to drive in other real-life situations, including driving at night or in the rain. When you are practicing how to drive, practice in as many real-life situations as possible while you have a licensed driver in the vehicle with you.

WHERE TO PRACTICE DRIVING

The best place to practice your basic skills during the first phase of your driving practice is an open area, like a parking lot, so that you can learn the basics without having to navigate around other vehicles. This has been a starting location for so many new drivers for a reason. Along with providing an open place to practice, another benefit to practicing in a parking lot are the painted lines, which can be great for honing in on your skills, as well as be a guide to you as you practice.

Driving in these more secluded areas will not only help you gain confidence and get comfortable behind the wheel, but it will also allow you more reaction time between each scenario you wouldn't otherwise have if you jump right into practice on the road surrounded by traffic and other obstacles.

After you have mastered the basics in a parking lot, the next phase of practicing is getting onto the road. To help ease into this, start in a quiet neighborhood or low-traffic back road. This will allow you the space to practice basic skills without the stress of busy, fast-paced roads. Selecting less populated roads also allows you some grace for basic learner mistakes without as much risk of hurting yourself or other people. Ideally, you want to start in an area where the speed limit is 25 mph and then increase your speeds as you build confidence.

It's a good idea to plan out your route or see it before you drive it. This will help make sure that you know what to expect and eliminate some of the surprises in your first driving lesson. Whether it is your route to school or driving to a familiar location, this will help make the transition from the safety of your parking lot or driveway to the road a lot easier.

After getting onto the road, if you feel that you are not entirely comfortable with the foundational skills of driving a vehicle, it is okay to return to a secluded spot, like a parking lot, to practice some more. This is not only to help you gain confidence in your driving abilities but also to ensure that you are staying safe while driving a car.

Along with practicing in different driving conditions, driving on different types of roads and areas is crucial in making sure that you are prepared for any driving situation when you get out onto the road on your own. Driving in your neighborhood is very different from driving through a rural town, into an urban city, or on a major highway. Getting practice in all of these areas or on all of these types of roads will make sure that you are ready for any situation that you might encounter while you are driving.

It is also beneficial to practice driving in snow and on ice in the event that you need to drive in these conditions. Practicing this skill in an empty parking lot or frozen lake allows for plenty of space to practice these skills without other vehicles or other obstacles to worry about. When driving on ice, you should focus on braking slowly with little traction, accelerating slowly, and steering with very controlled movements.

Take Your Time!

The amount of time in the first phase is critical and depends on the person. We all learn how to drive at our own pace, so if it takes you a little bit longer to master the basics and feel comfortable with the essential functions of driving a car, that's okay! The responsibility of driving a vehicle is essential, not only for your own safety, but for the protection of the other drivers, bikers, and pedestrians on the road. Getting on the road too early can be dangerous, so make sure that you are entirely comfortable with all of the basic functions of a vehicle before you get onto the open road.

When you are practicing driving, it is crucial to listen to the person who is teaching you to drive during these sessions. It can be difficult at times, especially if things go wrong, but those teachable moments are when your teacher can guide you the most. Be open to conversations about your driving, both during and after your driving practice tests. It is through this feedback that you will learn more about what you should and should not be doing while you are driving.

When we are young, we feel like we are invincible and know almost everything. When you begin driving, make sure that you are listening to the licensed driver. Believe it or not, they do know better than you do when it comes to driving.

Going back to the basics is not something that you should ever feel ashamed of, but instead, should feel proud of. When you are driving, it is a huge responsibility, and knowing when you need to go back to the basics is the responsible thing for you to do. When in doubt, go back to the basics. Those basics are the foundation of what you are going to be doing.

Remember, there is no such thing as too much practice. The more time that you put into practicing driving in each stage will help you to be a good driver, as well as a safe driver. Knowing your limitations is another critical part of learning how to drive. Do not try to take on too much at one time, as this could lead to costly mistakes.

Everyone learns things at their own pace, and there is no set guide on when you might be ready to go to the next step of learning how to drive. While learning and comparing notes with your peers is exciting, remember that you might all be at different stages, and that is okay!

Once you receive your learner's permit, each state requires a specific number of hours of practice driving before earning your license. A good way to earn these hours is by driving to certain things each day, like school or work. If you can get more than the minimum required hours, even better. After all, practice makes perfect!

After earning your driver's license, you'll no longer be required to ride with someone else. Make sure to take advantage of this time to have guidance and instant feedback regarding your driving skills. This will help you become a more confident and safer driver in the long run.

YOUR DRIVER'S LICENSE

Getting your driver's license is an exciting time, but the process can be daunting and challenging to understand. A driver's license is required to authorize you to operate a vehicle. Getting a driver's license is required in every state if you want to drive a car, and it is earned after proving you understand the laws of the road, as well as competency behind the wheel.

The general process for getting your license is the same in every state. You will begin by taking a test to obtain your learner's permit. Once you have received your learner's permit, you will need to complete a minimum number of required practice hours. In most states, these hours will also require a specific number of nighttime driving hours to complete before you can take your driver's test. After completing the requirements, you will take an on-the-road driving test to earn a provisional license.

Below you will find the requirements for each state as of the time of the publication of this book. It is a good idea to double check your state's guidelines. This is only a basic reference.

Alabama

- You can apply for your learner's permit at 15-years-old.
- 50 hours of driving practice is required before applying for your license.
- A driver's education course is not required in Alabama to receive your driver's license.
- Alabama requires a road skill test and a restricted driver's license at age 16.
- You can apply for an unrestricted license after six months with the restricted license.

Alaska

- You must be between fourteen and sixteen years old to get your instruction permit after passing a written test, a vision test, and getting parental consent.
- You are required to practice driving for six months with an instructional permit before applying for your license.
- Alaska requires 40 hours of practice time before applying for a license.

- A driver's education course is not required in Alaska to receive your driver's license.
- At sixteen years old, you can apply for a provisional license.
- At 18-years-old, you are able to apply for a non-provisional license.

Arizona

- You must be at least fifteen years and six months old to get your instruction permit after passing a written test and a vision test.
- You must drive with an instruction permit for at least six months.
- You must complete a minimum of thirty hours of driving practice, including ten night-time practice hours with a licensed driver.
- A driver's education course is not required in Arizona to receive your driver's license.
- If you complete a driver's education course, you are not required to take a road test to get your license.

Arkansas

- You must be at least fourteen to fifteen years old to get your learner's license after passing a written test, a vision test, and getting parental consent.
- You must drive with an instruction permit for at least six months.
- You must complete a minimum of forty hours of driving practice, including ten practice hours in challenging conditions with a licensed driver.

- A driver's education course is not required in Arkansas to receive your driver's license.
- At sixteen years old, you will take a road skill test at your local Department of Motor Vehicles office to get your provisional driver's license.
- Once you have turned eighteen years old, you can receive your non-provisional driver's license.

California

- You must be at least fifteen years and six months old to get your instruction permit after passing a written test and a vision test.
- You must drive with an instruction permit for at least six months.
- You must complete a minimum of fifteen hours of driving practice, including ten night-time practice hours with a licensed driver.
- A driver's education course is required in the state of California to receive your driver's license.
- At sixteen years old, you will take a road skill test at your local Department of Motor Vehicles office to get your provisional driver's license.
- Once you have turned eighteen years old, you can receive your non-provisional driver's license.

Colorado

- You must be at least fifteen years old to get your instruction permit after completing a thirty-hour driver's education class before passing a written test.

- You must drive with an instruction permit for at least six months.
- You must complete a minimum of fifty hours of driving practice, including ten night-time practice hours with a licensed driver.
- A driver's education course is required in Colorado to receive your driver's license.

At sixteen years old, you will take a road skill test at your local Department of Motor Vehicles office to get your driver's license.

Connecticut

- You must be at least sixteen years old to get your instruction permit after passing a written test and a vision test.
- You must drive with an instruction permit for at least six months.
- You must complete a minimum of forty hours of driving practice with a licensed driver.
- A driver's education course is required in Connecticut to receive your driver's license.
- At sixteen years old, you will take a road skill test at your local Department of Motor Vehicles office to get your driver's license.

Delaware

- You must be at least sixteen years old to get your learner's permit after completing a driver's education class before passing a written test.
- You must drive with an instruction permit for twelve months. During the first six months, you

cannot drive unsupervised; however, after the first six months, you can drive unsupervised.

- You must complete a minimum of fifty hours of driving practice, including ten night-time practice hours with a licensed driver.
- A driver's education course is required in Delaware to receive your driver's license.

Florida

- You must be at least fifteen years old to get your learner's permit after passing a written test and a vision test.
- You must practice driving with your permit for at least a year.
- You must complete a minimum of fifty hours of driving practice, including ten night-time practice hours with a licensed driver.
- A driver's education course is required in Florida to receive your driver's license.
- At sixteen years old, you will take a road skill test at your local Department of Motor Vehicles office to get your driver's license.

Georgia

- You must be at least fifteen years old to get your instruction permit after passing a written and vision test.
- You must practice driving with your permit for at least a year.

- You must complete a minimum of fifty hours of driving practice, including ten night-time practice hours with a licensed driver.
- Before receiving your provisional license, you are required to complete an Alcohol and Drug Awareness Program.
- A driver's education course is also required in Georgia to receive your driver's license.
- At sixteen years old, you will take a road skill test at your local Department of Motor Vehicles office to get your driver's license.

Hawaii

- You must be at least fifteen years old to get your instruction permit after passing a written and vision test.
- You must drive with an instruction permit for at least one year.
- You must complete a minimum of fifty hours of driving practice, including ten night-time practice hours with a licensed driver.
- A driver's education course is required in Hawaii to receive your driver's license.
- At sixteen years old, you will take a road skill test at your local Department of Motor Vehicles office to get your driver's license.

Idaho

- You must be at least fourteen years and six months old to get your instruction permit after completing a thirty-hour driver's education class before passing a written test.

- You must drive with an instruction permit for at least six months.
- You must complete a minimum of fifty hours of driving practice, including ten night-time practice hours with a licensed driver.
- A driver's education course is required in Idaho to receive your driver's license.
- At fifteen years old, you will take a road skill test at your local Department of Motor Vehicles office to get your driver's license.

Illinois

- You must be at least fifteen years old to get your instructional permit after you have passed a written and vision test.
- You must drive with an instruction permit for at least nine months.
- You must complete a minimum of fifty hours of driving practice, including ten night-time practice hours with a licensed driver.
- A driver's education course is required in Illinois to receive your driver's license.
- After having your instructional permit for nine months, you will take a road skill test at your local Department of Motor Vehicles to get your driver's license.

Indiana

- You must be at least fifteen years old with a driver's education class or sixteen years old without a driver's education class to get your learner's permit after passing a written and vision test.
- You must drive with an instruction permit for at least six months.
- You must complete a minimum of fifty hours of driving practice, including ten night-time practice hours with a licensed driver.
- A driver's education course is not required in Indiana to receive your driver's license.
- After six months of driving with your learner's permit, you will take a road skill test at your local Department of Motor Vehicles office to get your driver's license.

Iowa

- You must be at least fourteen years old to get your instruction permit after completing a driver's education class before passing a written test and vision test.
- You must drive with a learner's permit for at least one year.
- You must complete a minimum of twenty hours of driving practice, including two night-time practice hours with a licensed driver.
- A driver's education course is required in Iowa to receive your driver's license.

- At sixteen years old, you will take a road skill test at your local Department of Motor Vehicles office to get your driver's license.

Kansas

- You must be at least fourteen years old to get your instruction permit after completing a thirty-hour driver's education class before passing a written test.
- You must drive with an instruction permit for at least one year.
- You must complete a minimum of fifty hours of driving practice, including ten night-time practice hours with a licensed driver.
- A driver's education course is required in Kansas to receive your driver's license.
- After driving with your learner's permit for one year, you will take a road skill test at your local Department of Motor Vehicles office to get your driver's license.

Kentucky

- You must be at least sixteen years old to get your instruction permit after completing a thirty-hour driver's education class before passing a written test.
- You must drive with an instruction permit for at least six months.
- You must complete a minimum of sixty hours of driving practice, including ten night-time practice hours with a licensed driver.

- A driver's education course is required in Kentucky to receive your driver's license.
- After six months of driving with your instructional permit, you will take a road skill test at your local Department of Motor Vehicles office to get your driver's license.

Louisiana

- You must be at least fifteen years old to get your instructional permit after completing a driver's education class and then passing a written test.
- You must drive with an instruction permit for at least six months.
- You must complete a minimum of fifty hours of driving practice, including fifteen night-time practice hours with a licensed driver.
- A driver's education course is required in Louisiana to receive your driver's license.
- After six months with your instructional permit, you will take a road skill test at your local Department of Motor Vehicles office to get your driver's license.

Maine

- You must be at least fifteen years old to get your learner's permit after passing a written test.
- Six months of driving practice with a learner's permit is required before applying for a license.
- You must complete a minimum of seventy hours of driving practice, including ten night-time practice hours with a licensed driver.

- A driver's education course is required in Maine to receive your driver's license.
- After six months with your learner's permit, you will take a road skill test at your local Department of Motor Vehicles office to get your driver's license.

Maryland

- You must be at least fifteen years and nine months old to get your learner's permit after passing a written test.
- You must drive with a learner's permit for at least nine months.
- You must complete a minimum of sixty hours of driving practice, including ten night-time practice hours with a licensed driver.
- A driver's education course is required in Maryland to receive your driver's license.
- After nine months of driving with your learner's permit, you will take a road skill test at your local Department of Motor Vehicles office to get your driver's license.

Massachusetts

- You must be at least sixteen years old to get your learner's permit after passing a driver's education course and a written test.
- You must drive with a learner's permit for at least six months.
- You must complete a minimum of forty hours of driving practice with a licensed driver.

- A driver's education course is required in Massachusetts to receive your driver's license.
- After six months of driving with your learner's permit, you will take a road skill test at your local Department of Motor Vehicles office to get your driver's license.

Michigan

- You must be at least fourteen years and eight months old to get your learner's permit after passing both a driver's education course and a written test.
- You must drive with a learner's permit for at least six months.
- You must complete a minimum of fifty hours of driving practice, including ten night-time practice hours with a licensed driver.
- A driver's education course is required in Michigan to receive your driver's license.

After six months of driving with your learner's permit, you will take a road skill test at your local Department of Motor Vehicles office to get your driver's license.

Minnesota

- You must be at least fifteen years old to get your learner's permit after passing both a driver's education course and a written test.
- You must drive with a learner's permit for at least six months.

- You must complete a minimum of fifty hours of driving practice, including fifteen night-time practice hours with a licensed driver.
- A driver's education course is required in Minnesota to receive your driver's license.
- After six months of driving with your learner's permit, you will take a road skill test at your local Department of Motor Vehicles office to get your driver's license.

Mississippi

- You must be at least fifteen years old to get your learner's permit after passing a written test.
- You must drive with a learner's permit for at least one year.
- A driver's education course is not required in Mississippi to receive your driver's license.
- After one year of driving with your learner's permit, you will take a road skill test at your local Department of Motor Vehicles office to get your driver's license.

Missouri

- You must be at least fifteen years old to get your learner's permit after passing a written test.
- You must drive with a learner's permit for at least six months.
- You must complete a minimum of forty hours of driving practice, including ten night-time practice hours with a licensed driver.

- A driver's education course is not required in Missouri to receive your driver's license.
- After six months of driving with your learner's permit, you will take a road skill test at your local Department of Motor Vehicles office to get your driver's license.

Montana

- You must be at least fourteen years and six months old to get your learner's permit after passing both a driver's education course and a written test.
- You must drive with a learner's permit for at least six months.
- You must complete a minimum of fifty hours of driving practice, including ten night-time practice hours with a licensed driver.
- A driver's education course is not required in Montana to receive your driver's license.
- After six months of driving with your learner's permit, you will take a road skill test at your local Department of Motor Vehicles office to get your driver's license.

Nebraska

- You must be at least fifteen years old to get your learner's permit after passing a written test.
- You must drive with a learner's permit for at least six months.
- You must complete a minimum of fifty hours of driving practice, including ten night-time practice hours with a licensed driver.

- A driver's education course is not required in Nebraska to receive your driver's license.
- After six months of driving with your learner's permit, you will take a road skill test at your local Department of Motor Vehicles office to get your driver's license.

Nevada

- You must be at least fifteen years and six months old to get your learner's permit after passing a written test.
- You must drive with a learner's permit for at least six months.
- You must complete a minimum of fifty hours of driving practice, including ten night-time practice hours with a licensed driver.
- A driver's education course is required in Nevada to receive your driver's license.
- After six months of driving with your learner's permit, you will take a road skill test at your local Department of Motor Vehicles office to get your driver's license.

New Hampshire

- You must be at least fifteen years and six months old to get your learner's permit after passing a written test.
- You must complete a minimum of forty hours of driving practice, including ten night-time practice hours with a licensed driver.

- A driver's education course is not required in New Hampshire to receive your driver's license.

New Jersey

- You must be at least sixteen years old to get your learner's permit after passing driver's education and a written test.
- You must drive with a learner's permit for at least six months.
- A driver's education course is required in New Jersey to receive your driver's license.
- After six months of driving with your learner's permit, you will take a road skill test at your local Department of Motor Vehicles office to get your driver's license.

New Mexico

- You must be at least fifteen years old to get your learner's permit after passing a written test.
- You must drive with a learner's permit for at least six months.
- You must complete a minimum of fifty hours of driving practice, including ten night-time practice hours with a licensed driver.
- A driver's education course is required in New Mexico to receive your driver's license.
- After six months of driving with your learner's permit, you will take a road skill test at your local Department of Motor Vehicles office to get your provisional driver's license.

- A year with a provisional license is required before applying for an unrestricted driver license.

New York

- You must be at least sixteen years old to get your learner's permit after passing a written test.
- You must drive with a learner's permit for at least six months.
- You must complete a minimum of fifty hours of driving practice, including ten night-time practice hours with a licensed driver.
- A driver's education course is not required in New York to receive your driver's license. However, if you do not take a driver's education course, you will need to drive with a provisional license for an additional year.
- After six months of driving with your learner's permit, you will take a road skill test at your local Department of Motor Vehicles office to get your provisional driver's license.
- After you have had your provisional driver's license for six months, you will be eligible for an unrestricted driver's license with a driver's education class or one year and six months without a driver's education class.

North Carolina

- You must be at least fifteen years old to get your learner's permit after passing a written test.
- You must drive with a learner's permit for at least one year.

- You must complete a minimum of sixty hours of driving practice, including ten night-time practice hours with a licensed driver.
- A driver's education course is required in North Carolina to receive your driver's license.
- After six months of driving with your learner's permit, you will take a road skill test at your local Department of Motor Vehicles office to get your provisional driver's license.
- Once you have turned eighteen years old, you will be able to drive in North Carolina on an unrestricted driver's license.

North Dakota

- You must be at least fourteen years old to get your learner's permit after passing a written test.
- If you are younger than 16-years-old, you are required to practice driving with a learner's permit for a year before applying for your license. For those ages 16-18, you are only required to hold a learner's permit for six months before applying for a license.
- You must complete a minimum of fifty hours of driving practice with a licensed driver.
- A driver's education course is required in North Dakota to receive your driver's license.
- After six months of driving with your learner's permit, you will take a road skill test at your local Department of Motor Vehicles office to get your provisional driver's license.

- You will be eligible for an unrestricted driver's license after you turn sixteen years old once you have met all the requirements for a learner's permit.

Ohio

- You must be at least fifteen years and six months old to get your learner's permit after passing a written test.
- You must drive with a learner's permit for at least six months.
- You must complete a minimum of fifty hours of driving practice, including ten night-time practice hours with a licensed driver.
- A driver's education course is required in Ohio to receive your driver's license.
- After six months of driving with your learner's permit, you will take a road skill test at your local Department of Motor Vehicles office to get your provisional driver's license.
- After you turn eighteen years old, you will be eligible for an unrestricted driver's license.

Oklahoma

- You must be at least fifteen years and six months old if you have taken a driver's education class, or sixteen years old without having taken a driver's education class to get your learner's permit after passing a written test.
- You must drive with a learner's permit for at least six months.

- You must complete a minimum of fifty hours of driving practice, including ten night-time practice hours with a licensed driver.
- A driver's education course is not required in Oklahoma to receive your driver's license.
- After six months of driving with your learner's permit, you will take a road skill test at your local Department of Motor Vehicles office to get your provisional driver's license.
- After you have had your provisional driver's license for six months, you will be eligible for an unrestricted driver's license.

Oregon

- You must be at least fifteen years old to get your learner's permit after passing a written test.
- You must drive with a learner's permit for at least six months.
- You must complete a minimum of fifty hours of driving practice with a licensed driver if you are enrolled in a driver's education class or one hundred hours of driving practice with a licensed driver if you are not enrolled in a driver's education class.
- A driver's education course is not required in Oregon to receive your driver's license.
- After six months of driving with your learner's permit, and when you are at least sixteen years old, you will take a road skill test at your local Department of Motor Vehicles office to get your provisional driver's license.

- After you have had your provisional driver's license for at least one year, you will be eligible for an unrestricted driver's license.

Pennsylvania

- You must be at least sixteen years old to get your learner's permit after passing a written test.
- You must drive with a learner's permit for at least six months.
- You must complete a minimum of sixty-five hours of driving practice, including ten night-time practice hours and five hours practicing in inclement weather with a licensed driver.
- A driver's education course is required in Pennsylvania to receive your driver's license.
- After six months of driving with your learner's permit, you will take a road skill test at your local Department of Motor Vehicles office to get your provisional driver's license.

Rhode Island

- You must be at least sixteen years old to get your learner's permit after passing a written test.
- You must drive with a learner's permit for at least six months.
- You must complete a minimum of fifty hours of driving practice, including ten night-time practice hours with a licensed driver.
- A driver's education course is required in Rhode Island to receive your driver's license.

- After six months of driving with your learner's permit, you will take a road skill test at your local Department of Motor Vehicles office to get your provisional driver's license.
- After you have had your provisional driver's license for at least one year, you will be eligible for an unrestricted driver's license.

South Carolina

- You must be at least fifteen years old to get your learner's permit after passing a written test.
- You must drive with a learner's permit for at least six months.
- You must complete a minimum of forty hours of driving practice, including ten night-time practice hours with a licensed driver.
- A driver's education course is required in South Carolina to receive your driver's license.
- After six months of driving with your learner's permit, you will take a road skill test at your local Department of Motor Vehicles office to get your provisional driver's license.
- After you have had your provisional driver's license for at least one year, you will be eligible for an unrestricted driver's license.

South Dakota

- You must be at least fourteen years old to get your learner's permit after passing a written test.

- You must drive with a learner's permit for at least six months with a driver's education class or nine months without taking a driver's education class.
- You must complete a minimum of fifty hours of driving practice, including ten night-time practice hours and ten practice hours in inclement weather with a licensed driver.
- A driver's education course is not required in South Dakota to receive your driver's license.
- After six months of driving with your learner's permit, if you have taken a driver's education class, or nine months of driving with your learner's permit without having taken a driver's education class, you will take a road skill test at your local Department of Motor Vehicles office to get your provisional driver's license.
- After you turn sixteen years old, you will be eligible for an unrestricted driver's license.

Tennessee

- You must be at least fifteen years old to get your learner's permit after passing a written test.
- You must drive with a learner's permit for at least six months.
- You must complete a minimum of fifty hours of driving practice, including at least ten night-time practice hours with a licensed driver.
- A driver's education course is not required in Tennessee to receive your driver's license.
- After six months of driving with your learner's permit, you will take a road skill test at your local

Department of Motor Vehicles office to get your provisional driver's license.

- After you have had your provisional driver's license for at least one year, you will be eligible for an unrestricted driver's license.

Texas

- You must be at least fifteen years old to get your learner's permit after passing a written test.
- You must drive with a learner's permit for at least six months.
- You must complete a minimum of thirty hours of driving practice, including at least ten night-time practice hours with a licensed driver.
- A driver's education course is required in Texas to receive your driver's license.
- After six months of driving with your learner's permit, you will take a road skill test at your local Department of Motor Vehicles office to get your provisional driver's license.
- After you turn eighteen years old, you will be eligible for an unrestricted driver's license.

Utah

- You must be at least fifteen years old to get your learner's permit after passing a written test.
- You must drive with a learner's permit for at least six months.
- You must complete a minimum of forty hours of driving practice, including at least ten night-time practice hours with a licensed driver.

- A driver's education course is required in Utah to receive your driver's license.
- After six months of driving with your learner's permit, you will take a road skill test at your local Department of Motor Vehicles office to get your provisional driver's license.
- You will be eligible for an unrestricted driver's license after holding your provisional license for six months.

Vermont

- You must be at least fifteen years old to get your learner's permit after passing a written test.
- You must drive with a learner's permit for at least one year.
- You must complete a minimum of forty hours of driving practice, including at least ten night-time practice hours with a licensed driver.
- A driver's education course is required in Vermont to receive your driver's license.
- After one year of driving with your learner's permit, you will take a road skill test at your local Department of Motor Vehicles office to get your provisional driver's license.
- After you turn eighteen years old, you will be eligible for an unrestricted driver's license.

Virginia

- You must be at least fifteen years and six months old to get your learner's permit after passing a written test.

- You must drive with a learner's permit for at least nine months.
- You must complete a minimum of forty-five hours of driving practice, including at least fifteen night-time practice hours with a licensed driver.
- A driver's education course is required in Virginia to receive your driver's license.
- After nine months of driving with your learner's permit, you will take a road skill test at your local Department of Motor Vehicles office to get your provisional driver's license.
- After you turn eighteen years old, you will be eligible for an unrestricted driver's license.

Washington

- You must be at least fifteen years old if you are enrolled in a driver's education class or fifteen years and six months old if you are not enrolled in a driver's education class to get your learner's permit after passing a written test.
- You must drive with a learner's permit for at least six months.
- You must complete a minimum of forty hours of driving practice, including at least ten night-time practice hours with a licensed driver.
- A driver's education course is required in Washington to receive your driver's license.
- After six months of driving with your learner's permit, you will take a road skill test at your local Department of Motor Vehicles office to get your provisional driver's license.

- After you have turned seventeen years old, you will be eligible for an unrestricted driver's license.

West Virginia

- You must be at least fifteen years old to get your learner's permit after passing a written test.
- You must drive with a learner's permit for at least six months.
- You must complete a minimum of fifty hours of driving practice, including at least night-time practice hours with a licensed driver.
- A driver's education course is not required in West Virginia to receive your driver's license.
- After six months of driving with your learner's permit, you will take a road skill test at your local Department of Motor Vehicles office to get your provisional driver's license.
- After you turn seventeen years old, you will be eligible for an unrestricted driver's license.

Wisconsin

- You must be at least fifteen years and six months old to get your learner's permit after passing a written test.
- You must drive with a learner's permit for at least six months.
- You must complete a minimum of thirty hours of driving practice, including at least ten night-time practice hours with a licensed driver.
- A driver's education course is required in Wisconsin to receive your driver's license.

- After six months of driving with your learner's permit, you will take a road skill test at your local Department of Motor Vehicles office to get your provisional driver's license.
- After you turn eighteen years old, you will be eligible for an unrestricted driver's license.

Wyoming

- You must be at least fifteen years old to get your learner's permit after passing a written test.
- You must drive with a learner's permit for at least ten days.
- You must complete a minimum of fifty hours of driving practice, including at least ten night-time practice hours with a licensed driver.
- A driver's education course is not required in Wyoming to receive your driver's license.
- After you turn sixteen years old, you will take a road skill test at your local Department of Motor Vehicles office to get your provisional driver's license.
- After you turn sixteen years and nine months old, if you have taken a driver's education class or seventeen years old without having taken a driver's education class, you will be eligible for an unrestricted driver's license.

Several states require a driver's education course before earning your permit or license. Although there are online classes available, not all states accept these, so it is ideal to contact your local DMV before investing in these options.

Earning your driver's license is a significant milestone, and it is important to learn the rules, regulations, and processes associated with getting your driver's license. Each state is going to be slightly different, so make sure to look at the Department of Motor Vehicles website for your state to ensure that you are completing all of the requirements that you need to become a licensed driver.

THE DRIVER'S LICENSE TEST

What is the Driver's License Test?

When earning your driver's license, there are multiple tests required. The process starts with an instructional permit and a vision test. From there, you will earn a provisional license before receiving your unrestricted license.

A written test on basic road rules, insurance questions, and signage is required before receiving your learner's permit. The written test is taken at the local DMV and is usually timed. For most states, if you fail the written test, you are required to wait a specific number of weeks before trying again. If this happens, it is nothing to be ashamed of—it's fairly common to need to retake the written exam and is just an indication you need to study a little bit more.

You can easily find your state's driver's manual and practice tests for the written learner's permit test on your state's DMV website. As you prepare to take the written test to get your learner's permit, make sure that you study your state's driver's manual thoroughly so that you know and understand all of the rules and regulations of the road in that state. Taking practice tests will also be helpful by helping you get a feel for the types of information and questions that will be included on the written test for your learner's permit.

After you have taken the test and gotten your learner's permit, you will have a specific time frame and other requirements that you must meet before moving onto the next stage of the graduated licensing process. In order to get on the road with your provisional driver's license, you will take the driver's road test at your local Department of Motor Vehicles office. During this test, you will drive in a designated area and be tested on your ability to follow the rules of the road in realistic situations, as well as to show your ability to operate and control a vehicle.

WHAT TO KNOW BEFORE YOUR TEST

When you take your driving road test to get your provisional driver's license, the things that you will do during the test are similar in most states. There may be some variations in the things that you will be asked to do during the road test, depending on the state that you are taking the test in.

During the driver's license road test, you will be driving in a vehicle with a test examiner from the Department of Motor Vehicles, as well as driving through various real-life situations to show your skills and abilities on the road. During this test, you may be on a course, on the road, or a combination of the two. Where you will be driving during your driver's license road test depends on the office of the Department of Motor Vehicles that you are taking your test at. Common things that you will be tested on during your driver's test include driving in reverse, turning, passing through an intersection, three-point turns, changing lanes, and in some states you will be tested on your ability to parallel park. As you practice driving before taking the driver's license road test, make sure that you practice each of these skills and are comfortable with these skills.

When you are driving in reverse, you will begin by keeping your right foot on the brake pedal while shifting the vehicle into reverse. Place your hand on the upper-middle section of your steering wheel, look behind the car over the passenger side shoulder, and slowly take your foot off of the brake pedal, allowing the vehicle to move slowly. It is important to keep in mind that while you are driving in reverse, using your mirrors, as well as looking behind you is crucial to make sure that you are aware of any obstacles that may be behind you.

When making turns on your driver's license road test, go slow and keep your eyes on the road and vehicles around you. Using your turn signal is important to signal to those around you of your intention to turn right or left. While turning, you should keep your hands in the ten o'clock and two o'clock position, turning the wheel with a hand over hand motion to maintain control of the steering wheel.

There are many things to keep in mind when passing through an intersection. As you approach, slow down early enough to avoid an abrupt stop. Make sure you have the right of way before moving into the intersection. Even if you have the right of way, you still need to pay attention to other drivers and oncoming traffic. Just like when crossing as a pedestrian, you need to look both ways before entering the intersection. Despite the rules of the road, mistakes happen, and the test proctor will pay attention to how aware of your surroundings you are.

When passing another vehicle on the road, scan your surroundings for any hazards, such as oncoming traffic, merging vehicles, or vehicles approaching from the rear. Left lanes are considered the passing lane, while the right lane is considered the slow lane. It is important to check your mirrors and blind spots before using your turn signal and accelerating to pass. Once ahead of the vehicle that you are trying to pass, use your turn signal to return to the right lane.

There are several states that will require you to successfully complete a three-point turn to pass your driver's license road test. Like anything you do while driving, before you complete a three-point turn, make sure to use your turn signal to signal your intentions and check the road for hazards. When you are completing a three-point turn, the process varies, depending on your surroundings.

If you are completing a three-point turn while on an open road, turn the wheel completely to the left, and move across the road. After turning as far left as you can, put the vehicle into reverse and turn the wheel to the right as you back up your vehicle to clear whatever is in front of you. Next, return your vehicle to drive and straighten out by turning your wheel back to the left while slowly accelerating. It will take practice to smoothly straighten out your vehicle into the correct lane.

If you are completing a three-point turn with a parking space or in a course for your driver's license road test, you will begin by driving the vehicle past the parking space that you plan to use for your three-point turn. Once you have passed the parking space and determined there is enough room to park, put the vehicle in reverse, turn your wheel to the left, and back into the parking space. Finally, once you have successfully backed into the parking space, put the vehicle back into drive, check the road in front of you for hazards, and pull the vehicle out into the appropriate lane.

Parallel parking is something that some states will test you on during your driver's license road test and is one of the most common fears for new drivers getting ready for their test.

In order to parallel park, you will begin by positioning your vehicle so that it is parallel to the vehicle that is parked in front of the empty space that you are trying to park in. When you are parallel parking, make sure that you are using your turn signal throughout the process to indicate to other drivers that you are going to be entering the space. Once you are in position, check your mirrors, put the vehicle in reverse, check for any hazards, and begin backing up slowly with your steering wheel turned to the left side of the vehicle.

While backing up the vehicle, once you have entered the space that you are trying to parallel park in, you will turn your steering wheel to the right to ease the rest of your vehicle into the parking space. Line the center of your car up to the bumper of the vehicle in front of you. Turn your wheel to the left as you straighten your vehicle into the parking space. After backing into the parking space, you will make adjustments to fit properly into the space. There should be a comfortable amount of space in front of and behind you. Although this figure varies depending on state requirements, in general, you should be 10 inches away from the curbside.

While you are taking your driver's license road test, there are some states that will test your ability to drive on a freeway. During this part of the test, they will be testing your ability to safely enter and exit the highway, as well as passing other vehicles on a highway. The specific things that you will be tested on for your driver's license test depends on the location of the Department of Motor Vehicles that you are taking your driver's license road test, and the requirements of the state where you are trying to get your driver's license.

As you go through all of the steps of the driver's license test, the test examiner will be observing your ability to handle the vehicle safely and follow the rules of the road. The test examiner will also use this time to observe you using your turn signals, accelerating and braking, checking your mirrors, maintaining a safe following distance from other vehicles, and obeying speed limits.

PASSING YOUR DRIVING LICENSE TEST

Before you are able to get behind the wheel and begin your driver's license test, the test examiner will complete a safety inspection of your vehicle before your road test. They will check your lights and signals to make sure they are functioning properly as well as your tires and windshield. It is important your windshield is relatively free of distracting cracks and chips that might obscure your vision while driving.

Once your vehicle passes the safety inspection, the examiner will ask you to demonstrate your knowledge on various things, such as signals, windshield wipers, and lights. If you cannot show that you know the vehicle controls well, you will not pass your road test.

The test examiner may also ask you about turning on your turn signals, turning on the windshield wipers, turning on your emergency flashers, and checking your mirrors to ensure that they are adjusted properly. After you have proven that you know the controls of the vehicle, you will begin the driving portion of the driver's test.

Some states will have you begin your driver's test in a parking lot or on a driving course to show your basic skills before getting onto a public roadway. This is where you may be tested on skills, such as a three-point turn or parallel parking. Once you have finished with this part of the test, you will drive in another location, such as on a residential street or a main road so that the test examiner can observe your driving skills in real life scenarios.

To ease your nerves and help you pass your driver's test, try to practice driving the roads that surround the department of motor vehicles so that you are comfortable with all of the road signs you may be asked about. Know the speed limits of those streets and look for any obstacles that you might encounter while taking your driver's license road test.

While you are taking your driver's license road test, it is important to keep all of the rules of the road in mind, and make sure that you are following those rules throughout the duration of your road test. It's extremely important to use your turn signal with every turn that you take, maintain the appropriate speed limit and frequently check your mirrors to keep an eye on your vehicle placement and surroundings.

While you are driving with the test examiner, they will be focused on observing and grading your actions, so it is important to remain calm, and follow any instructions that the test examiner may give you. The test examiner may ask you questions about the things you see as you are driving, such as road signs, at various points throughout the test. While you are taking the test, stay calm. The test examiner is not rooting for you to fail, so if you are ever unclear on an instruction that they give you, just ask them!

The best way to pass your driver's license road test is to practice. Make sure that during your time driving with a licensed driver you are practicing as many scenarios as possible and practicing those scenarios as many times as possible. It is through repetition and practice that you will be able to get through your driver's license road test and pass it on the first try.

BEFORE YOU HIT THE ROAD

As discussed in the previous chapter, during your driver's license test, the examiner will complete a safety inspection. When you first begin driving, you will need to complete a more comprehensive check of your vehicle every time you get into the car; however, as you gain more experience behind the wheel and more experience with your vehicle, the thoroughness of your pre-driving check will be reduced, and you will get used to checking the necessary parts of your vehicle at regular intervals.

BEFORE GETTING INTO THE CAR

As a new driver, start by checking the outside of the vehicle. Check to make sure that your tires have the appropriate air and pressure. There is an inexpensive tool that you can purchase at most gas stations and automotive shops to check this. It's also a good idea to give them a quick look over for any visible damage. You can generally find the appropriate PSI levels for your tires on a sticker in the driver's side door frame of your car.

When checking the air pressure on your tires, you will remove the valve stem cap on the tire. This is in the outer rim of the tires hubcap and is a small tube with a cap on the end. Once you have removed the valve stem cap make sure that you put it in a safe location. You will then take the tire gauge and push the round end into the tire's valve stem. When you have pushed the tire gauge onto the valve stem, you should hear a faint rush of air that is pushing into the tire gauge. The tire gauge will then read a number, showing the PSI of the tire. This number may be digital or could be manual with a measure rod that comes out of the opposite end of the tire pressure gauge. If you are using a manual tire gauge, the largest number that is showing on the measuring stick is the current PSI level of the tire. After reading the tire pressure level, make sure that you replace the valve stem cap.

You should also take this time to check the tread on your tires and make sure that there is enough tread left on them to safely drive the car. You can use a tread depth gauge or if you do not have a tire tread gauge you can use a penny to check the tread on your tires. A tire depth gauge will mark where the treads should be to be safe to drive, but if you do need to use a penny, you can put the penny upside down between the tread grooves. If the tire tread covers the top of Lincoln's head, that means that there is enough tread left on your tires to be able to drive on them safely. If you can see the top of Lincoln's head, or there is a space above his head, that means that the tire treads are worn out. In which case, they are not safe to drive on and need to be replaced.

After making sure that your tires have enough tread left and are safe to be driven on, you need to check your windshield for chips and cracks. If there are chips or cracks on your windshield, this will obstruct your view as you are driving, and it is dangerous. Small chips are easy and safe to fix. It is important to fix them before they split into full cracks, which are more difficult to repair. Next, you'll check your lights for full function and clarity. Sometimes you'll need to clean or defog the glass over the headlights for optimal visibility at night.

Finally, you will want to take a quick look under the vehicle to make sure that there are no fluid leaks. If there are issues with fluid leaks, it could be an issue with oil dripping, or even your coolant or transmission fluid. If anything is leaking, this means that there could be an issue with your engine, and your vehicle will need to be looked at by a mechanic as soon as possible. If you notice that fluid is leaking from your car, do not drive the vehicle anywhere but a mechanics shop. Ignoring a fluid leak could lead to costly repairs or dangerous breakdowns while you are driving.

Once you have thoroughly checked the exterior of the vehicle to make sure that everything is functioning properly and that there is no damage that will be an obstruction or danger to your driving, it is time to get into the car. When you get into the vehicle, you will first want to buckle your seatbelt, make any seat adjustments, and adjust the mirrors as necessary.

After you have driven a vehicle and adjusted the mirrors, it is unlikely that you will need to adjust them again unless another driver has used the vehicle and adjusted them. Either way, it is important to always check to make sure that you are able to see each of the mirrors properly to drive safely.

Check for any lights on your dashboard to make sure that there are no warning lights on that need to be addressed, ensure there is plenty of gas in the vehicle, and that all of the gauges are functioning properly. Make sure you can comfortably reach the pedals and that they work. You can easily adjust your seat or even add a pillow as necessary.

BUCKLE UP!

After you have checked over your vehicle and made sure that the vehicle is safe and ready to drive, make sure that you buckle your seatbelt before putting the car in gear and pulling out onto the road. Putting on your seatbelt is a very simple thing to do and is one of the most important things that you can do. If you are in an accident, your seatbelt can save your life.

When putting on your seatbelt, make sure that the lower belt is sitting flat across your waist, and the upper part of the seatbelt is sitting flat across the middle of your chest, over your shoulder, and away from your neck. At all times, make sure that your seatbelt is not tucked under your arm or placed behind your back. The placement of your seatbelt is so important, as incorrect placement can result in an injury or even death if you are in a car accident.

If you drive without wearing your seatbelt, you are putting yourself at risk of severe injury from the airbag if you are in a crash, or even possibly being ejected from the vehicle completely. If you do not wear your seatbelt, whether you stay in the vehicle or if you are ejected from the vehicle, you are risking not only getting severely injured, but also death.

As the driver of the vehicle, you are also responsible for each of the passengers that are riding in your vehicle. When you get into the vehicle, after you have buckled your seatbelt, make sure that all passengers of the vehicle are in their seats and buckled up properly before you ever move the vehicle. Studies have shown that any passengers who are in the back seat of the vehicle are three times more likely to die in an accident if they are not wearing their seatbelt.

As the driver of the vehicle, if you get into an accident and something happens to your passengers, you are the one who can be held liable for their injuries. Every time that you get into the car, make sure that all of your passengers are buckled up and drive safely.

REMEMBER THE ESSENTIALS

When you are getting ready to leave and drive out on the open road, always make sure to check your brakes and mirrors one last time. If there are issues with your brakes or mirrors, this is putting you at significant risk of getting into an accident.

Your rearview mirror should be adjusted so that you can see out of the middle of your back windshield, and you should be able to do this without having to move your head around while sitting in the driver's seat. Your rearview mirror will be key in making sure that you can see the road and vehicles behind you without having to move around or turn. You should be able to quickly glance in this mirror to check for other vehicles around you.

Check and adjust your mirrors so you can see the road and other vehicles on either side of you. On the driver's side, you should be able to look in the side view mirror and see the road behind you and a small sliver of the driver's side of your vehicle. You would do the same process for the passenger side mirror, making sure that you could see behind your vehicle on the passenger side and a small sliver of the passenger side of your vehicle.

Finally, check your brakes. While the vehicle is in park, press down on the brake pedal to make sure that the brake pedal is working properly, and that the brakes are gripping properly.

Knowing the vehicle that you are driving is essential to staying safe while you are on the road. Making sure that your vehicle is in proper working order is essential to your ability to drive well, stay safe, and keep your passengers safe. Before you get into a vehicle, you should make sure that you know of any issues beforehand so that those issues can be taken care of quickly.

WHAT NOT TO DO WHILE DRIVING

In today's world, multitasking is a common theme through almost all parts of our lives, but driving should never be one of those places that multitasking lives. Attempting to multitask in any form while driving leads to unsafe activities that could easily lead to an accident. You will hear people tell you all the time not to look at your phone or try to do anything else while you are driving, make sure that you listen to them!

While it is very important to know the ins and outs of what you should do while driving, it is just as important to know what you should not be doing while you are driving. Knowing what you should not do while you are driving helps to make sure that you know what to look out for and avoid so you can be the best driver you can be. The best way to avoid certain behaviors is to recognize what those behaviors are in the first place. You may not think adjusting the radio is causing a distraction while you are driving, but it is, and when you recognize that, you are more cognizant of that distraction when you are going down the road.

ROAD LAWS ARE THERE FOR A REASON

Every state has created its own laws for driving on its roadways to make sure that the drivers that are on their roads stay safe. Most states have common laws when it comes to the rules of the road, but there may be additional laws that are specific to an individual state. When you do get your learner's permit, the written test works to test your knowledge of the rules of the road, including common road laws and road laws that are specific to the state that you are taking the test in. Taking this test should not be the end of your interactions with the rules of the road. If you are driving, knowing the rules of the road not only keep you from getting pulled over, but also help you prevent an accident. Make sure that you are keeping up with any new rules of the road as they are implemented in your state.

Every state does have a law in which both drivers and passengers are required to wear a seatbelt while in a moving vehicle. There are several states where you can get pulled over specifically for not wearing a seatbelt, while there are other states that will only ticket you for not wearing a seatbelt if you have been pulled over for something else. Regardless of the laws in your state, it is critical for you to wear a seatbelt every time that you get into a car. If you do not wear a seatbelt every time you get into a vehicle, you are putting yourself at risk of severe injury or even death in the event of an accident.

If you are on the road and there is an emergency vehicle approaching your location with its lights and sirens on, pull over, if possible, and let the emergency vehicle pass. Emergency vehicles, such as ambulances, fire trucks, or police cars move at very high speeds when they are in route to an emergency or transporting someone to a hospital. If you do not get out of the way of an emergency vehicle that is running with its lights and sirens on, you are putting yourself and the other vehicle at risk for a severe accident. In the event of an emergency, time is of the essence when an emergency vehicle is traveling to the scene, and if you do not move out of the way, you are also putting those who are involved in the emergency at risk if emergency service personnel do not arrive quickly.

In every state, you have to stop for school buses whenever their lights are on. Even if you are on the opposite side of the street, you must stop whenever buses turn their lights on. This helps protect students crossing the street or offloading and unloading from the bus. The only time it is okay not to stop is if there is a median separating you from the bus.

It is also a good idea to proceed with extreme caution if you see a school bus, regardless of whether the lights are on or not, as children will sometimes move into the roadway before the bus has gotten to the bus stop and is has come to a complete stop. If you do not come to a complete stop for a school bus, you are putting the children trying to get on or get off of the bus at risk of severe injury or death if you were to hit them.

While you are driving, it is important to make sure that you do not speed when you are driving. The posted speed limit has been put into place very specifically based on the road, the type of traffic on that road, and any other obstacles that are present on that road specifically. Driving the speed limit is essential to making sure that you are able to handle any obstacles that are on the road, and that you can successfully navigate the roadway without losing control of the vehicle.

When you first begin driving, it is important to learn as much as you can about the road laws in your state to make sure that you are staying safe and protecting others on the road around you as well. There are a lot of rules, but all are essential for new drivers, ensuring that there are no accidents, which may lead to severe injury or even death for the driver, as well as other drivers.

BECOMING THE SAFEST DRIVER POSSIBLE

While you are driving, it is important to make sure that you are keeping both hands on the steering wheel at all times. Both of your hands should be on each side of the steering wheel; oftentimes described to be at the nine o'clock and three o'clock position. Depending on the age of the person that is teaching you to drive, they may tell you to keep your hands in the ten o'clock and two o'clock position. This has been recently updated to help keep you safe, in the event that you are in an accident and your air bag deploys. Essentially, this means that you should have your hands on the right and left sides of the steering wheel.

While you are driving, make sure that you are keeping a firm grip on the steering wheel so that you can maintain control of the vehicle at all times. You should also make sure that you are gripping the steering wheel on the outside of the wheel, with the pressure mostly on your fingers and your thumbs should be pointed upwards. Keeping your hands on the inside of the steering wheel could lead to significant injuries if the air bag does deploy.

As you are driving a vehicle, it is also important to keep your posture in mind, focusing on how your body is positioned in the vehicle and your hand placement on the steering wheel. Not only do these things make it more comfortable for you while driving, but it helps with maintaining control of the vehicle and makes you less likely to get into an accident. While looking at car accidents in which a vehicle ran off the road, it has been found that improperly holding the steering wheel is commonly a main reason for those accidents.

Along with making sure that you have proper hand placement on the steering wheel, making sure that the steering wheel is at the appropriate height for you while driving is just as important. The steering wheel should be at a comfortable level that allows you to comfortably move the steering wheel without straining with it too high or hitting your legs because it's positioned too low. If you do need to adjust the height of the steering wheel when you get into the car, there is generally going to be a handle, or a lever, located underneath the steering wheel that you would use to move the steering column up or down.

DISTRACTED DRIVING

Driving in any manner that takes your attention away from the road is what is known as distracted driving. As you are driving, there are a number of things that you need to be paying attention to, and if you are focused on changing the radio station, texting your friends back or talking to the person in the passenger seat, you are not able to pay attention to everything that you need to while driving.

Cell phones have become such an integral part of society, and it can often be difficult to put them away or ignore it when they go off. This is one of the most common distractors for drivers and is a common reason for accidents. If you are going to use your phone for GPS, invest in a handless device. These usually attach to the dashboard. It is a good idea to put your phone on silent to avoid being distracted by incoming calls or texts. Although it's best to avoid taking calls while driving, if you must, use wireless devices to do so. Do not text and drive. It only takes a second with your eyes off the road for something to happen. Remember, you are traveling at fast speeds, and anything could happen. Whether it's an animal crossing your path or the car in front of you slamming on the brakes, you need to keep alert with your hands ready to react appropriately.

Using your cell phone is not the only thing that is dangerous to focus on while driving. Anything that distracts you from the road is dangerous and puts you at risk for an accident, which can cause severe injury, or even death. In today's society, cell phones are a more common distraction; however, changing the radio station, talking to the person in the passenger seat, eating, putting on makeup, or anything else that takes your attention away from the road is distracted driving. Many states have tried to put laws in place to try to get rid of distracted driving by banning cell phone use while behind the wheel. This is still something that is common. If you do use your cell phone while driving, you also risk getting pulled over and getting a ticket.

DON'T DRIVE TIRED

We have all had those days where we did not sleep well, or it's been a long day at work, and you just can't seem to keep your eyes open. If you drive while you are feeling tired or even to the level of being exhausted, you are at significant risk of getting into an accident. This is not only due to your risk of falling asleep at the wheel, but being tired has impacts on your cognitive abilities as well. When you are driving while tired, your reaction time is significantly slower and there is a possibility of dozing off, even for a few seconds. If you doze off while driving, it is easy for you to collide with another vehicle or run your vehicle off the road. A lot can happen in just a few seconds that will change the rest of your life or even the life of someone you've never met.

While analyzing the effects of sleep deprivation and exhaustion, it has been shown that the mental impairment that people show is similar to severe intoxication from drugs or alcohol. The impairment of being exhausted makes you more likely to be distracted, slows down your reaction time, and makes you less attentive to your surroundings. If you are feeling tired or exhausted, take the nearest exit and pull off the road and rest. It could save your life and the life of others.

While you are driving, you need to make sure that you are staying attentive to the road and staying cautious with how you drive to protect yourself, your passengers, and the other people that are on the road with you. Make sure to follow all of the rules of the road at all times, eliminate distractions, such as the radio or conversations with passengers, and put your phone away. Anything that takes attention away from the road puts you at risk of an accident, which can mean severe injury or death for yourself or other drivers on the road.

ACCIDENTS

You hear people talking about accidents all the time or see stories of accidents on the news. Whether they saw one on the road, are telling the story, or if someone who is teaching you how to drive is having a conversation about being a safe driver, accidents are something that you will always hear about. As and the effects that a car accident can have is an important part of becoming a safe driver, knowledge is power, and knowing what you are trying to avoid can help keep you alert to the dangers of the road while you are driving.

What is an Accident?

A car accident is when a vehicle collides with something else, such as another vehicle, an animal that is in the road, other road debris, pedestrians, or any other obstruction in or near the road. A car accident not only risks injury or death for anyone who is involved, but getting into a car accident is also costly in terms of damage to your vehicle or property damage that occurs from the accident.

There are a wide variety of reasons that a person may get into an accident, including speed, weather, impairment, aggressive driving, or distracted driving, just to name a few. A car accident is something that is most commonly unintentional in nature but can have catastrophic results for anyone and everyone who is involved.

PREVENTING ACCIDENTS

While you are driving, there are a wide variety of things that you can do in order to help prevent a car accident from happening. In order to help prevent an accident, it is important to eliminate as many of the distractions as possible, and drive as safely as you can.

Aggressive driving can cause an accident if you are tailgating or speeding. Tailgating is where you or another driver are driving extremely close to the vehicle that you are following. Tailgating can often lead to a rear-end collision if the vehicle in front of you needs to make a sudden stop. Speeding is also dangerous, and is almost just as dangerous as tailgating, as the higher the speed you are traveling, the more likely you might be to lose control of the vehicle. The speed limits for a specific road have been posted for specific reasons, and following those speed limits is an important part of staying safe and preventing an accident.

While driving, it is important to follow what any road signs and signals that are present are telling you. Drivers who run a stop sign or a traffic light can cause accidents, and this could also include those who do not come to a complete stop when approaching traffic lights and stop signs before continuing into the intersection. When you come up to a traffic light or a stop sign, make sure to come to a complete stop at the stop line or cross walk, and look both ways before carefully accelerating and passing through the intersection.

An important part of preventing car accidents is making sure that you have a clear mind before ever getting behind the wheel of a car. A significant number of car accidents occur every year when the driver of one of the vehicles is under the influence of drugs or alcohol. Being impaired by these substances causes lower reaction times, may lower your ability to concentrate on the road, and can have an impact on your overall coordination. Never get behind the wheel of a car while under the influence of drugs or alcohol, even if you don't feel impaired. You may be more cognitively impaired than you realize and cause an accident. If you need to get somewhere while under the influence call a trusted friend or cab service to get you where you need to go. If you get behind the wheel while under the influence, you are putting yourself and everyone around you in danger. You should also never get in a vehicle with someone who is under the influence of drugs or alcohol, no matter how many times they might tell you that they are fine.

Distracted driving is becoming an increased reason for car accidents. Distracted driving could be changing the radio station, using your cell phone, talking to someone in the passenger seat or eating. Make sure that you do not use your phone while driving and keep it out of reach to reduce temptation. Make sure to change the radio station before you begin driving the vehicle, and do not eat while you are driving. These are all ways that you can avoid distracted driving and help prevent a car accident.

While driving, make sure to keep a safe distance between you and other vehicles. This will protect you if traffic stops suddenly or you need to react to an accident. You cannot control other drivers and anything can happen on the road. If you follow too closely, you will not have enough time to react. Some example situations that can occur include someone popping a tire and swerving out of control, a driver falling asleep at the wheel or swerving under the influence, a vehicle's brakes failing, or an animal running into the road.

Any time that you are behind the wheel of a car, make sure that you are paying attention to all other vehicles around you, and keep yourself safe by avoiding any situations that could cause you to suddenly slam your brakes or swerve while driving down the road. If you notice that another driver is driving in an erratic or unsafe manner, distance yourself from that vehicle as quickly as possible.

Try to avoid driving at night when at all possible, and if you have to drive at night, try to make sure that you are driving on well-lit roads. Driving at night, regardless of how good your vision might be, it is going to be more difficult to see things around you, especially if you are driving in bad weather at the same time. When it is more difficult to see an obstacle in the road, the more likely you are to collide with that obstacle, getting yourself into a bad accident. When driving at night, both you and the other drivers on the road are also going to be more tired than you would be while driving during the day. While driving tired, driving is more dangerous as your reaction times are slower and you are likely to doze off behind the wheel.

Along with avoiding driving at night, stay off the road during times of inclement weather if it is possible. If you are driving in the rain or snow, it is more difficult to see out of the windshield as the rain or snow hits it. During times of inclement weather, it is also a possibility that you could lose traction while traveling down the road. Losing traction means that the tires are unable to grip the road, and this leads to the vehicle sliding and becoming uncontrollable. If you do need to drive in inclement weather, make sure to drive slowly, use both the brake pedal and gas pedals gently, and make sure that you are leaving some extra distance between your vehicle and the other vehicles that are around you.

Keeping total control of your vehicle and concentrating on the road and everything around you are two of the ways that you can work to prevent a car accident from happening. This is an essential skill and is a primary part of being a safe driver, while protecting yourself, your passengers, and other people who are around while you are driving.

TYPES OF ACCIDENTS

There are several different types of accidents that happen on the road on a daily basis. Each of them are based on the premise of a collision, but each also inflicts their own damage to all that are involved in the accident. The different types of car accidents include rear-end collisions, head-on collisions, roadway departure crashes, rollovers, and side collisions.

A rear-end collision is something that you see referred to as a fender bender or rear-ending someone. This type of collision happens when the front bumper of a vehicle crashes into the rear bumper of the vehicle that is in front of it. A rear-end collision is one of the most common types of collisions and can happen for a variety of reasons, including sudden stopping, distracted driving, or even bad weather when a vehicle loses traction on the road. This type of collision can vary widely with regard to the amount of damage that is caused during the accident, which could include minimal damage, such as a small dent on the bumper, or significant damage if the vehicle in the back is moving at a high speed at the time of the collision. When it comes to a rear-end collision, oftentimes the following driver is held liable for the collision, which is another reason that maintaining a safe following distance is critical when you are driving.

A head-on collision is a crash in which something hits the vehicles directly in the front, head-on. This type of collision could be a collision with another vehicle that is travelling in the opposite direction or it could be with a stationary object, such as a guardrail, telephone pole, or even a tree. This is one of the most dangerous types of accidents as the driver is generally moving at a higher rate of speed and can also happen if you are accidentally driving the wrong way on a one-way street or if you end up on the wrong side of the road.

A roadway departure collision is an accident that occurs when a vehicle goes off the designated roadway. This type of car accident occurs if the driver cannot fully control the vehicle, whether it be because of impaired driving, distracted driving, road conditions, or even vehicle system failure. In a roadway departure collision, once the vehicle goes off of the road, it collides with something else, which could result in a totaled vehicle. In a roadway departure collision, the vehicle is remaining upright, but is no longer in the road.

A rollover collision, on the other hand, is a crash when a vehicle turns on its side or on its roof due to the collision. During a rollover collision, the vehicle may turn once or could roll multiple times before landing in its final position on its side or roof. Rollover collisions happen when the vehicle tips over another object, such as a guardrail, and sometimes happen if the vehicle is going too fast around a turn or is hit on the side from another vehicle. This is the most dangerous type of car accident and can result in a person being ejected from the vehicle or trapped in the vehicle, leading to severe injury or death.

A side collision is an accident in which the side of the vehicle is impacted, which most commonly occur at intersections or in parking lots. This is often referred to as a T-bone accident because one vehicle collides into the side of another, forming the shape of a T. These accidents commonly happen because of a distracted driver or a driver running and failing to stop at a traffic signal that has turned red or at a stop sign.

Whether the car accident occurs on a highway, country back road, or any other type of roadway, they all have risks for injury or death, not only to you, but anyone else that might be involved in the collision.

WHAT TO DO WHEN AN ACCIDENT HAPPENS

When you are behind the wheel of a car, you have a significant responsibility to keep yourself, your passengers, and the other people on the road as safe as you possibly can. Like in everything else in life, accidents do happen, and if you are involved in an accident, it is important to keep that in mind. You are not a failure, and you are not the worst person--it was an accident!

When we are talking specifically about a car accident, we are talking about a vehicle colliding with another object. That object could be another car or could be other obstacles, such as an animal, a tree, or a building. No matter what the obstacle is that you get into an accident with, it is important to remain calm and remember that it's an accident and accidents do happen.

While an accident is serious and can cause serious injury or even death, getting into an accident is just that, an accident. If you have gotten into an accident, you may be shaken up and that is completely normal. Take a deep breath and calm yourself down before trying to assess the situation and follow the steps that you need to when an accident has occurred.

WHAT TO DO IF YOU'RE IN AN ACCIDENT

If you do get into a car accident, there are a few things that you need to do. First things first, you need to make sure that you and your passenger(s) are okay. If you or your passenger(s) are injured in the car accident, call 911 or get someone else to call 911 for you if you are unable to do so. If there are any serious injuries, it is important to make sure that the person who is injured does not move until emergency personnel arrive to assess the situation.

If you are able to move safely, get away from the vehicle and to a safe place, such as a sidewalk or off to the side of the road. In the event of an accident, your vehicle will be stopped while everything is handled and getting to a safe area is important to avoid another vehicle hitting your stopped vehicle or having something happen to your vehicle, which could be dangerous if you are near.

Make sure that if you are in a car accident, you do not leave the scene. If you do need to move to a safe location, make sure that you are still near the location of the accident. If you leave the scene of an accident, you could face criminal charges for fleeing the scene, lose your driver's license, and even lose your insurance coverage.

Regardless of the type of accident that you are in, whether it was a fender-bender or a more serious accident, such as a head-on collision or a rollover collision, you should always call the police afterwards. This will help to provide any documentation that you may need for insurance and in some states, it is legally required that police are called to the scene of an accident. Make sure to keep a copy of the police report from the accident in case it is needed as documentation in anything related to the accident, such as an insurance claim.

Not only will a police officer create an accident report about the collision, but the officer that responds to the scene will also check over those individuals that were involved in the accident to make sure that there are no significant injuries and call for emergency medical technicians, if necessary. The police officer will also investigate the circumstances of the accident to determine which driver was at-fault for the accident and may also issue a ticket to the driver who is found to be at-fault for the collision.

After you have made sure that everyone that was involved in the accident is okay and you have spoken with the police, it is time to take photos of the accident as additional documentation for your insurance company. Make sure that you take photos of both vehicles, any damage to either of the vehicles involved, photos of any property damage, such as a guardrail or other damaged property, and, if necessary, any injuries that were sustained during the accident. It also may be helpful to take photos of the road and general area where the accident was located.

CALLING YOUR INSURANCE COMPANY

When you have been in an accident, you will need to exchange contact information, along with insurance information with the other driver that was involved in the accident. When exchanging this information, make sure to include your name, phone number, insurance company name, policy number, license plate numbers and the make, model, and color of the damaged vehicles involved. When getting information from the other driver, make sure that you are also getting the same information in return. The police may also include all of this information in the accident report to make sure that everyone has all of the necessary details.

Insurance is an important part of driving a vehicle, and in many states it is required before you are able to operate a vehicle. As soon as possible after the accident, make sure to file a claim with your car insurance company, providing as much documentation as possible. After you have filed a claim with your insurance company, the insurance adjuster will review all of the documentation that has been provided to determine who is at-fault for the accident and any coverage that may be required for the accident.

If possible, try to contact your insurance company while you are at the scene of the accident. While you are talking to your insurance company, the insurance representative that you are speaking to will tell you all of the documentation that they will need to have while they are investigating and processing your claim. Make sure that all documentation that they require is submitted as quickly as possible to help avoid any possible delays in the claims process.

The vehicle claims process will take longer when submitting the appropriate documentation after the accident. Make sure that you are keeping a record of everything that goes along with the accident in case you need to reference it in the future, in case the insurance company has questions during the investigation and processing of the claim.

WHAT TO DO IF YOUR CAR BREAKS DOWN

Even if you are not in an accident, things can happen to your vehicle suddenly and your car might break down. Simply put, when your car breaks down, that means that your car stops working for some reason or another. This could be a mechanical failure of the engine, an issue with the electronics of the vehicle, or any number of systems in your vehicle, all of which can impact the ability for your car to run.

Your car can break down at any point, which is why regular maintenance and checking over your vehicle regularly is so important. Catching anything that could go wrong before it happens allows you to address the problems ahead of time and can save you from breaking down on the side of the road.

WHY CARS BREAK DOWN

There are several common reasons for a car breaking down, including problems with your tires, battery issues, if your engine has overheated, brake issues, and transmission issues. Some of these problems you may be able to address on your own in the event of a breakdown, while others you may need to call a mechanic or tow company for assistance.

Tire issues are a common reason for a car to break down and could include a flat tire or even a tire blowout. A flat tire is when your tire loses air pressure over time and the tire does not have enough air in it to move safely, if it has any air in it at all. When you have a flat tire, the vehicle is riding either on just the tread of the tires or even just the rim of the tire, depending on how low the tire pressure has gotten. On the other hand, a tire blowout is when the tire suddenly loses all tire pressure, sometimes in an explosive moment. If you have issues with your tires, it is important to make sure that you are out of any lanes of traffic before assessing and addressing the issue.

Battery issues are another reason for a vehicle breakdown; however, unlike tires, these are more likely to happen before leaving an area that you had the vehicle parked. There are a number of reasons that your battery might die, such as leaving your headlights on, not closing the door all the way so the interior lights of the vehicle do not turn off, or any other accidents that lead to power being constantly drained over a longer period of time. Battery issues may also be caused by corrosion on the battery terminals. If you are unable to get the vehicle to start due to battery issues, check the battery for any corrosion and clean any corrosion before proceeding to jump start the vehicle.

If you do need to jump start the vehicle, you will need to make sure that you have another vehicle in which the battery is not dead and jumper cables to connect the battery of your vehicle to the battery of the vehicle that is being used to jump start. You will first need to make sure that both of the vehicles are facing each other so that the jumper cables are able to reach both sides. Once both vehicles are in the appropriate position, you will need to pop open the hood of both vehicles and locate the battery in each vehicle. You will begin by placing the red clamps to both vehicles, starting with the dead battery, and then connecting the other end to the vehicle that is jump starting the dead vehicle. You will then follow the same process for the black clamps on both vehicles, but this time you will first connect the black clamp to the negative post of the good battery and then finish the process by connecting the final black clamp to either a metallic part of the dead car's engine block or the negative post of the dead battery. It is not recommended that you connect the black clamp to the dead car's negative post, because this can cause what is called "sparking" After all of the clamps have been placed properly, begin by starting the vehicle with the good battery, give it a few minutes, and then try to start the battery of the dead vehicle.

There may be an issue with an overheated engine that causes your car to break down. While you are driving, there are a few things that you can look out for if your engine is overheating from problems like an oil or coolant leak. Check the dashboard for any warning lights and check the temperature gauge on your dash for any indications of the engine overheating. There may be some smoke or steam coming out from under the hood of the car, the hood may be hot to the touch, or even a potential for a loud clicking noise. Make sure that you never drive a vehicle that is overheating, as you can cause permanent damage to the engine or other systems in the car.

Brakes are something that you need to be careful with and can be a cause of a vehicle breakdown if you do not get them replaced regularly. If you begin to hear a squealing sound or a grinding sound while you apply the brakes, this is an indication that the brakes need to be replaced. If you do not get the brakes replaced regularly, this could lead to issues with them failing while you are driving, which is extremely dangerous. Every vehicle has a recommendation on how often the brakes should be replaced, so check out the vehicle manual to learn the recommendations for your specific car.

If you have issues with the transmission, this can cause a vehicle to suddenly stop driving. To avoid issues with the transmission, get regular oil changes and if you notice any weird noises, see fluid puddling under the vehicle, or if you notice a burning smell while you are driving, make sure to take your car into a shop to get it fixed immediately.

Always remember, checking and servicing the systems of your car regularly can help to prevent vehicle breakdowns and costly repairs. If you have questions about a system in your vehicle, hear a weird noise, or do not know how to check to see if something is functioning properly, take your vehicle to a trusted mechanic to get your car looked at and get any issues taken care of immediately.

STEPS FOR IF YOUR CAR BREAKS DOWN

If you do experience a vehicle breakdown, there are several steps that you should follow to make sure that you are staying safe and that the problem can be handled in the most appropriate way. If anything happens while you are driving, the first thing that you should do is turn on your hazard lights. The purpose of the hazard lights in your vehicle is to indicate that something has happened that is potentially dangerous and alerts drivers to proceed with caution while driving near the vehicle that has turned its hazard lights on.

After turning on your hazard lights, slow down and pull over to the side of the road, out of traffic. If you are on the highway or a crowded road, stay inside of the vehicle while you call for help. If you need to get out of your vehicle, you need to keep alert for traffic and make sure it is safe. While assessing the situation and calling for help, if necessary, make sure to stay a safe distance from the vehicle in case of a collision. Before getting out of the vehicle, be sure to check that the roadway is clear for you to exit the vehicle. If you do need to get out of the vehicle, it is safer to get out of the passenger door to stay away from the moving traffic that is passing on the driver's side.

When you do pullover, it is also a good idea to pull your parking brake to help prevent the car from rolling and creating an even more dangerous situation. You should also turn the wheel as far to the right as possible, causing the wheel to turn away from the road, which will help to keep the car from entering into the roadway if it does begin to roll. By doing this, if the car does begin to roll forward, it will roll off to the side of the road or into the ditch, rather than rolling into oncoming traffic.

After you have gotten to a safe location, call for help to get a mechanic, roadside assistance, or a tow truck. The person you will need to call depends on the type of breakdown that you are facing and the services that are available to you. If you are unsure of who you should contact or if you are dealing with an emergency situation, call the local police or 911. Some insurance policies include roadside assistance as a part of the policy. If you are unsure of your coverage, reach out to your insurance agent to find out more about what your policy.

Vehicles can have issues at any time. Breakdowns can be limited with proper maintenance and vehicle checks to ensure that things are running as they should be. However, if you do face issues with a vehicle breakdown, remain calm, get to a safe location, turn on your hazards and call for help.

ROAD SIGNS AND SPEED LIMITS

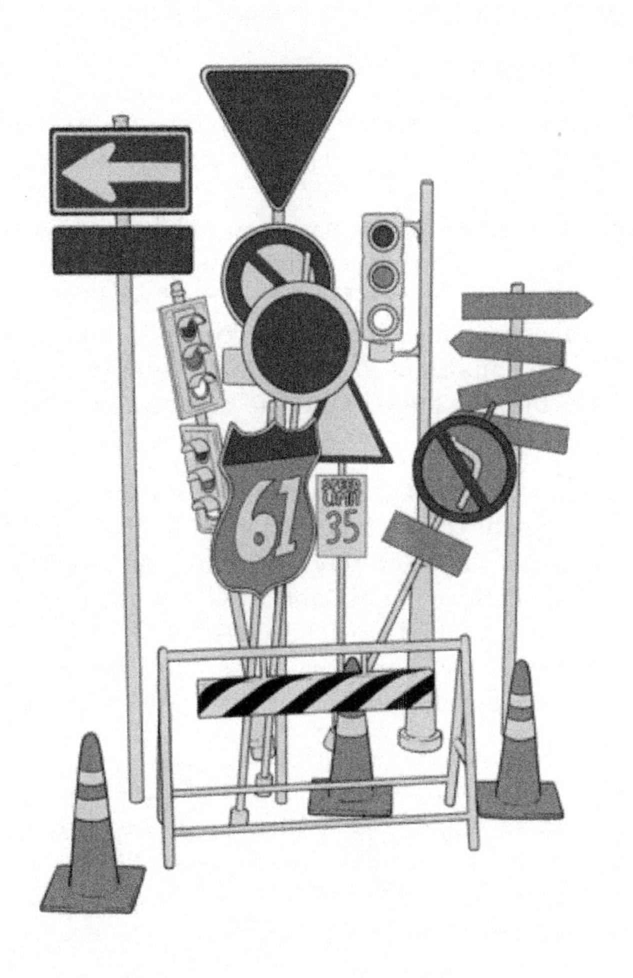

When you first begin driving, you take the written test about the rules of the road, along with questions about road signs, speed limits, and everything else that you need to know when you are driving to get your learner's permit. While it is important to know these things for that written test, road signs and speed limits are crucial things to know and follow while you are driving down the road, no matter how long you have been driving.

Road Signs

While driving down any government run road in any state, you will see signs that indicate the different expectations of drivers that are operating on that street. Road signs have been placed to tell both drivers and pedestrians things that you are allowed to do on that road things that you cannot do on that road, and information about the road and area where you are driving. As you drive, it is important to follow the directions of all road signs as they are there to keep all drivers and pedestrians safe.

The different road signs that you will see on the road will be in different colors, based on what that specific sign is trying to tell you. Red road signs are only used on stop signs, prohibitive signs, and yield signs. These signs indicate that immediate action needs to be taken by the driver to make sure that the driver is on the correct side of the road and that the driver is staying safe with other traffic.

Regulatory signs, such as speed limit signs and one-way signs, are in white, and tell the driver about the traffic laws in effect on that road, regulations, or even requirements that might apply at all times or at specified times on a road or highway. Yellow signs are used for more general warning messages, such as a bridge narrows sign, slippery road, or divided highway sign. Large orange signs on the side of the road indicate road work and guide drivers through any changed traffic patterns.

Brown signs are used to guide drivers and pedestrians to tourist destinations and public recreation areas. Along with signs to guide you to recreational sites, blue signs are used to guide drivers to rest areas, give tourist information, or guide drivers through evacuation routes.

Most road signs contain large images and limited writing to avoid any issues of a driver misinterpreting a road sign, which could cause a major accident. Studies have shown that symbols and images are easier to recognize, and at the same time work to close the communication gaps that are prevalent with the vast number of different languages that are present throughout the United States. This is something that is being adopted worldwide as diversity continues to spread.

With road signs primarily consisting of specific colors and images, there are many drivers who see the colors and symbols and do not need to examine the road sign to understand what the sign is indicating. This helps drivers keep their focus on the road ahead of them as they quickly identify the intended meaning of the road sign that they are driving past.

Speed Limits

Speed limits are posted on roadways and set the max speed that a driver should be traveling down a given stretch of road. The speed limit for a road shows the maximum speed that has been deemed as safe for a road with ideal weather and traffic conditions. There are several reasons that speed limits are set, and not just to keep control over people driving on the roads.

Having a set speed limit helps eliminate significant differences in the speed that the drivers are traveling, attempting to drive efficiently on the road. Speed limits also give drivers the ability to be safer when reacting to the actions of other drivers around them. Knowing the general speed of those around you helps you maintain a safe following distance, reduce the risk of accidentally tailgating another vehicle, and helps to reduce the number of crashes that happen on the road. Finally, the use of speed limits helps give police guidelines to help as they work to keep the public safe from reckless or negligent drivers.

While driving, it is important to keep in mind that speed limits are based on the road in ideal conditions and driving in inclement weather would mean driving at a slower speed to keep yourself and others on the road safe. If you are driving while the roads are wet, icy, or covered in snow, speeding can cause you to lose traction and cause your vehicle to go out of control and possibly slide into another vehicle. In inclement weather, all vehicles should be moving at a slower pace, and if the visibility in that weather is limited, hazard lights should be turned on as another way for a vehicle to be identified from a distance.

When you are behind the wheel, it is important to follow speed limits that have been posted. These speed limits are set in a way to keep you safe and reduce the number of accidents that occur on the road. Speed is one of the number one factors behind car accidents and following the posted speed limit is another way for you to help prevent an accident from occurring. Not only is the speed limit in place to help reduce accidents, but it is also illegal to speed. Avoid the speeding ticket, protect yourself and others, and help prevent accidents by following the posted speed limits.

RIGHT OF WAY LAWS

When you are driving, it is important to understand what right of way is and who has right of way in various real-life scenarios. Right of way refers to when a driver has the right to move first while in an intersection. If you have the right of way while driving, this means that you are the driver that is supposed to continue driving normally, while the person who does not have right of way must yield to the driver or pedestrian that does have right of way in that intersection.

If you do not follow the laws of right of way, you are risking a collision with another driver, a pedestrian, or even someone who is riding their bike on the same road as you. Right of way refers to the person who legally has the right to move first, and if you do not yield to another driver who has right of way and cause an accident, you will be held responsible as the at fault driver in that car accident.

If you are driving through an intersection that has traffic lights or stop signs, those signs determine who has the right of way for that intersection. If you are at an intersection that has a traffic light, the traffic light will tell you who has the right of way by the color that is lit on that traffic light. A green light means that you have right of way when it comes to going straight through an intersection, but you must yield while turning left or right to other vehicles that are approaching from the opposite direction. You would maintain the right of way while turning if you have a green arrow. If you are ever unsure of what a traffic signal means, look to see if there is additional signage that is posted that might be able to help guide you through that specific intersection.

If you are at an intersection that has stop signs, the vehicle that has gotten to the intersection first has the right of way to proceed through the intersection first. If two vehicles arrive at the intersection at the same time, the vehicle on the right-hand side has the right of way to go through the intersection first.

Whenever you are approaching an intersection, you should always yield to any cars, pedestrians or bikes that are already passing through the intersection. While most traditional intersections consist of two roads that intersect, T intersections are when the road that you are driving on ends into a through street. If you do get to a T intersection on the through street, continue driving as you normally would. On the other hand, if you approach a T intersection on the dead-end road, you will yield to the traffic that is passing on the through street on both the left and right sides.

You may also encounter an intersection where a smaller one or two-lane road intersects a larger road or highway. The larger highway has a higher speed limit, which makes it significantly more difficult to stop than a vehicle that is traveling on a smaller road with a lower speed limit. If you do encounter this type of intersection, the vehicle that is on the smaller road must yield the right of way to the vehicles that are on the larger road.

Some states do have different right of way laws, so when studying the laws of the road in your state as a new driver, make sure to check to see if there are any additional laws that might apply to you while driving. Not knowing the laws of the area where you are driving is not an excuse for causing an accident or injuring another person.

DRIVING IN DIFFERENT LOCATIONS

Depending on the area you are from, or how much you might travel, there are a wide variety of locations that you might find yourself driving in. Each of these different locations pose their own unique challenges when driving on these roadways. If you are going to be driving in a location that is new to you, it may be helpful to do some research about the appropriate ways to drive in that location to make sure that you are staying safe.

Where will you be driving?

One of the most common places that you might find yourself driving is in a neighborhood. These roads have lower speed limits, but have obstacles, such as pedestrians, parked vehicles, and bicycles that you need to keep an eye out for when you are driving. As you drive in neighborhoods, make sure that you are driving slowly, keeping your foot hovering over the brake pedal and staying extra careful when dealing with intersections, driveways, and other areas where people might be walking, or kids might be playing. If you do not stay extra careful when driving in a neighborhood, you could face devastating effects if you hit another vehicle or even a child.

If you live in a more rural area, you may be faced with driving on a back country road. These roads are travelled less often, and often have larger ditches and trees on either side of the road. If you are travelling on back roads, not only do you need to make sure that you are staying in your lane, but you will also need to make sure that you are keeping an eye out for wildlife that may enter the roadway. If you are unfamiliar with the area, it can be easy to get lost on back roads or lose GPS signal due to a lack of internet signal, so make sure that you have a map of the area in case you get lost.

Back roads may have more curves that you might not be used to if you have previously only been exposed to driving on city roads and highways, so make sure that you are driving slowly and keeping your eyes on the road for anything that might be an obstacle. You may also drive on a back roads in a mountain setting, which poses similar obstacles, but you are also facing the added challenge of driving on an incline or a decline.

If you are driving in a major city, there will be more traffic on the road, more pedestrians that you need to keep an eye out for, along with road work that might be occurring in various parts of the city or one-way streets. When driving in the city, make sure that you are driving slower and that you are covering the brakes while you are driving in the city. You should also make sure that you are reading every road sign carefully to avoid driving the wrong way down a one-way street or into a construction zone.

To cover your brakes means to keep your foot hovering over the brake pedal as you drive, ready to use the brake as needed. This is important in the city with the additional obstacles that you might face. With additional traffic and pedestrians, there is a higher likelihood that you might need to apply the brakes quicker than if you were driving on an open highway or back road.

The additional traffic that you will be facing when driving in the city can be stressful and there are a few things that you should keep in mind to make sure that you are staying safe. Make sure that you are using a navigation system, these are updated frequently and can reroute you if you miss a turn or if there is road work that you might encounter. Some of the newer navigation apps can also help to route you based on the traffic conditions that you might encounter while driving on a specific route. While managing the additional traffic of driving in the city, along with keeping an eye on the vehicle in front of you, make sure that you are also keeping an eye on the vehicles that are in front of that vehicle, and maintaining a safe following distance behind that vehicle.

Driving on highways, unlike driving in cities, involves driving at higher speeds, exit ramps, varying traffic patterns based on the location and time of day, and other driver's that can be unpredictable with the additional lanes of traffic. While driving on major highways, it is extremely important that you are staying alert and ready at all times and be ready to react as needed if other drivers are changing lanes erratically or if another vehicle has to make a sudden stop.

While driving on the highway, it is important to avoid "highway hypnosis" by keeping your eyes moving to different focal points on the highway that are around you. Highway hypnosis happens when a driver is driving on open highways for longer periods of time and the driver begins to drive the vehicle in a drowsy or trance-like state. This can lead to the driver falling asleep behind the wheel, which can lead to an accident. Taking frequent breaks while driving is important to make sure that you are not at risk of falling into highway hypnosis.

Whether you live in an arid climate or you are driving in the desert on a road trip, there are several things that you should know as a driver. Driving through the desert is a dangerous place and there are several things that you should do as a driver to make sure that you are staying safe and keeping your passengers safe as well. When driving through the desert, the pre-vehicle check is one of the most important things that you can do before getting on the road to drive through the desert.

One of the first things that you want to check is the tire pressure for your vehicle. When you are driving in hot temperatures, if your tire pressure is low, this can cause your tires to wear out quickly. The faster that your tires wear out, the more likely you are to experience a flat tire, or a tire blowout while you are driving in the desert. This can be particularly dangerous if you are in a desert climate away from other people. In case you do have a vehicle breakdown while in a secluded area, make sure that you have plenty of water in the vehicle, and a charger for your phone so that you can reach out for help if it is needed. If you do have a breakdown in a climate such as this one, do not leave the vehicle. These areas can span miles between people and buildings, so leaving your vehicle can leave you lost and reduce your chances of finding help.

WATCH OUT FOR PEDESTRIANS

When talking about pedestrians, we are talking about people who are walking along a road or who might be walking on a sidewalk in a more developed area like a city. We hope that pedestrians will stay out of the roadway, but as we all know, people are generally very unpredictable and while driving, you should always drive as if a pedestrian could walk out into the road at any minute.

If you are driving in a neighborhood, pedestrians may consist of people walking down the sidewalk, children playing in their yard or possibly in the street, or any other reasons that people may be moving near the road in their neighborhood. If a ball goes into a street, it is very possible that a child may dart into the road to retrieve it, or if a person needs to cross the street to their neighbor's house, you may not be able to see them around other vehicles that are parked on the side of the road. It is important to make sure that you are driving slowly and expecting these things to happen in order to keep everyone around you safe.

While you are driving through a city or small town, pedestrians are something that you should always be on the lookout for. Some states have laws that require the operator of a car to come to a complete stop for any pedestrians that are in the roadway. While there are generally a number of crosswalks on streets in both cities and towns, it is common to see pedestrians go into the road to cross the street outside of a cross walk.

If you are driving on a smaller back road or country road, you may encounter a bicycle rider or pedestrian on the side of the road. In this scenario, it is important to make sure that the roadway around you is clear of any dangers. Slow down, and give the pedestrian plenty of room as you pass. A general rule of thumb is to give at least three feet of distance between them and your vehicle to help reduce the risk of a collision with that pedestrian.

FINDING ALTERNATE ROUTES

When you are learning to drive, developing a route to practice on is going to be one of the first steps you take, but developing different routes that you might drive is something that you will never stop doing. Whether it is driving to school or work, to the mall in the next town over, or taking a weeklong road trip, developing your route is the first thing that you will do. By developing a route, you are able to see the way that you will be driving. This will not only help to keep you from getting lost, but this will also help you to prepare for any obstacles before you get to that area. Developing a route ahead of time is also something that is beneficial if you are going to be driving in a different climate or type of roadway that you haven't driven on before.

If you are planning your route, you have a lot of different options that are available to you to make sure that you are going in the right direction. For decades, people have used paper maps to find their way and this is still an option that is available to you. It is always a good idea to make sure that you have a paper map, even if you are using a GPS to guide you in case the battery dies or you are in a secluded location that does not have the appropriate service to continue to navigate you in that area. If you are planning a longer road trip, it is a good idea to have a paper map of the areas where you are driving in case something does end up happening.

There are several applications that you can use online as well to map a route ahead of time and print a copy of those directions. These programs, such as MapQuest, have been used by people for decades and are a great alternative if you cannot find a map of the area that you are traveling in or if you have a specific way that you need to be traveling for your trip. When using these programs, not only will it show you the route that you are going to take on a map, but it will also give you step-by-step instructions on how to get to your destination. If reading a map is something that you struggle with, having a map with the step-by-step instructions next to the map could be especially helpful in getting you to where you need to go.

If you are driving on your own on a longer trip, it is important to make sure that you are staying safe while driving. If you are using paper directions or if you lose GPS signal and need to begin using a paper map or a printout of directions, make sure that you pull over before attempting to read anything. If you do have a passenger with you, having the passenger assist with navigation while you are on the road is extremely helpful and helps reduce the distractions of trying to read the directions while driving on your own. If you do need to have a passenger navigate on your trip, talk to the navigating passenger before you begin driving on the expectations that you might have while they are navigating for you. This should include a conversation about the amount of time that you need to know about a turn prior to arriving at that turn, the noise level of the vehicle, making sure that you are on the same page in terms of the radio, and eliminating distractions for both yourself and the passenger that is helping to navigate.

If you are taking a shorter trip or if it is an everyday area that you are driving, using a GPS device, or even the map application on your cellphone is the most popular choice that people tend to use to navigate while they are driving on the road. If you do choose to use a GPS device or a maps application on your cell phone, it is important to make sure that the volume has been turned up so that you can hear the step-by-step instructions that you are getting from the program, and that it is mounted in a way that you can navigate without being on your phone. This will allow you to utilize these navigation features while limiting the distractions that you might be facing. It is also a good idea to put your phone on Do Not Disturb mode so that you are not tempted to check a text or answer a phone call while you are using your phone to navigate.

If you are navigating with a GPS, make sure that you have programmed the destination, adjusted the GPS settings, and checked the route before you begin driving. If you attempt to adjust anything with the GPS while you are driving, you are risking an accident by driving while distracted. If you do need to change the route while you are driving, make sure to pull over to the side of the road or into a nearby parking lot and put the vehicle in park before you begin to make any adjustments to the GPS. This not only makes sure that you are not driving while distracted by the changes that you are making to the route in your GPS, but this will also make sure that your vehicle does not roll accidentally while you are making adjustments.

No matter how you choose to select which route you are going to take to get to your destination, what the route is for, or how you are going to proceed along that route to get to your destination, it is important to make sure that you are staying safe. Another reason to outline your route before leaving is that it helps you to become familiar with the areas that you are going to be driving in case you have to deal with a vehicle breakdown or if the vehicle is disabled for any reason. If you get into an accident, any responders who you call for assistance will need to know your location to assist, and knowing your route ahead of time can help make sure that you know the location that they might need to respond to.

Making sure that there is enough time for your route will also assist in making sure that you are reducing stress, which in turn can mean reducing the risk of road rage and reckless driving. Knowing your route, the speed limits and obstacles on that route can make sure that you are more prepared for anything that you might encounter while driving on that specific route.

ROAD RAGE AND RECKLESS DRIVERS

When you are on the road, you are not only responsible for keeping yourself and your passengers safe with your own actions, but you also need to keep an eye on the other drivers that are around you as well. Whether it is handling the road rage of other drivers or other reckless drivers on the road, keeping an eye on their driving is crucial in making sure that you are able to react properly and that everyone is staying safe on the road.

As humans, it is normal to feel stressed or frustrated at times, which is a common reason that road rage incidents occur on the road every day. Whether you are the person that is dealing with road rage, or you are the victim of a road rage incident, there are several things that you can do to handle the situation.

WHAT IS ROAD RAGE?

When you are on the road, frustration can be a normal feeling, but some drivers experience what is known as road rage when that frustration leads to aggressive and potentially violent outbursts based on the frustration that someone is feeling while driving. There are a wide variety of ways that you might experience road rage, including screaming, making rude comments to another driver, or even threatening the other driver out of frustration.

Many people even report a driver driving in a way that is dangerous to themselves or others in an attempt to intimidate the other driver based on the frustration that they are feeling. These dangerous driving methods may include speeding, tailgating, cutting off another driver or brake checking a driver. Each of these may lead to an accident and could cause significant injuries or even death.

How to Handle Road Rage

If you are driving down the road and have a run in with a driver that is showing signs of road rage, there are a few things that you can do to help keep yourself and your passengers safe, as well as make sure that you are not escalating the situation. When in a situation that involves a driver with road rage, make sure to let that driver pass you and make sure to avoid any eye contact or gesturing towards that driver. If you do make eye contact with the driver or gesture in any way that would indicate your frustration, it can further escalate the situation, putting all parties involved in danger. Some drivers that are dealing with road rage may take this as a challenge, which in turn could lead to even more dangerous driving methods by that driver or even a confrontation if you end up next to that driver at a red light or stuck in traffic.

In recent years, there has been an uptick in road rage violence situations, including fights, intentional accidents, and even shootings. Just like in other parts of your life, if you are dealing with the rage of another person, letting the other person proceed with what they want to do may be the safest option. If you are driving and encounter another driver that is experiencing road rage, letting them proceed with their actions may be the safest thing for both you and your passengers. If the driver that is experiencing road rage is driving in a way that is dangerous for others on the road, you may consider pulling your vehicle over and reporting the aggressive driver to the authorities. This will help make sure that you are not personally escalating the situation, but helping to protect other drivers that may be a victim of a similar road rage incident that you just experienced.

If you are the driver that is experience road rage towards another driver, whether it is from frustrations outside of driving or a bad experience with another driver, it is important that you take steps to calm down and recompose yourself before continuing to drive.

If you are beginning to feel road rage, take a deep breath or even pull over to the side of the road to try to calm yourself down before proceeding. While you are driving, it may also be helpful to focus on the immediate things that are around you and where you are driving to. If you end up in a situation where you are stopped near the driver that was showing signs of road rage. Do not get out of your vehicle and make sure that your windows are rolled up and that the doors of your vehicle are locked.

WHAT IS A RECKLESS DRIVER?

When you are on the road, whether it is a situation involving road rage or not, reckless driving is something that you may encounter while driving down the road. When thinking about reckless driving, the easiest way it can be described is driving in a way that is dangerous, either to yourself, to others, or even for both. Reckless driving may be something that is intentional, or it may be something that the driver is not even realizing is happening, such as driving at a significantly higher speed than the posted speed limit.

One of the most common ways of reckless driving is speeding, and in most states, when you get to speeds between 15 and 20 miles over the speed limit, getting pulled over will also result in a citation for reckless driving, along with the general speeding ticket that you would receive during that traffic stop. When you are driving above speed limits, you are ignoring the established safety guidelines that the state has put into place, which is reckless. By traveling at higher speeds, especially if those speeds are significantly higher than those that are driving around you, is causing an increased danger of a collision for both yourself and the other vehicles that are on the road around you. You are also going to be at a higher risk for losing control of the vehicle that you are driving.

Another common way that a person may be driving recklessly is if they are not following the road signs, stop signs, or traffic signals that they come into contact with while driving down the road. The road signs that have been put on the road, as you have read about in previous chapters, are put on the road for a reason, and if a driver does not follow the guidelines that have been put into place with those road signs, they are causing a dangerous situation, whether it is intentional or not.

Rolling through a stop sign is a common way that people drive recklessly, and it is one that we may not think of when we first think about reckless driving. When a stop sign is placed on a road for an intersection, that means that there is traffic that is coming from different directions and drivers need to be aware of other drivers in that area, and make sure that the conditions for passing through that intersection are safe before proceeding.

If a driver does not come to a complete stop at a stop sign, that is limiting the amount of time that they are spending looking for other vehicles that are coming or even other obstacles that might be in the road, such as a pedestrian or a person that is riding a bicycle through the intersection. Not only would this limited amount of time lead to an increased likelihood of an accident, but this also reduces the reaction time that you may have while driving if you do happen to notice another vehicle or obstacle while proceeding through the intersection at the last minute.

Similar to stop signs, traffic lights have been added in specific locations for a purpose and each light that is on a traffic light has a specific purpose. If a driver does not follow the directions of the traffic light, they are putting both themselves and others in danger. A solid green light or a green arrow are the two indicators on a traffic light that mean to proceed through the intersection as the driver with the right of way at that time. If you approach a light that is yellow, this means to slow down and make a stop, or proceed with caution if you are at the point of no return when approaching that traffic light.

If you are approaching a traffic light as it turns yellow, begin to slow down and as you approach the intersection, make a stop at the red light that is coming quickly after. The only time that you should pass through a traffic light on a yellow light is if you are passed what is known as the point of no return. The point of no return is the point where you would not be able to safely stop the vehicle before entering the intersection while driving through the light. To stay safe, never accelerate quickly to get through a yellow light before you have approached the point of no return. This is something that you may see on the road, and it can be as dangerous as intentionally driving through a red light.

Whenever you are passing through an intersection, whether it is a stop sign or traffic light, think back to what your parents told you when you were growing up and crossing the street. Make sure that you are looking for other vehicles or other obstacles each way and then back again to make sure that the road is clear before you proceed into the roadway with caution.

Another example of reckless driving is driving while you are under the influence of drugs or alcohol. If you are under the influence of drugs or alcohol, your decision-making abilities are lowered, you have significantly slower reaction times than if you are sober minded, and you are less able to concentrate on the road and all of the things that require your attention while you are driving a vehicle. Getting behind the wheel of a vehicle while you are under the influence of drugs or alcohol is intentionally driving recklessly and could lead to yourself or others getting hurt or killed.

If you are on the road, there are a few signs that can help you identify a reckless driver who may be under the influence while behind the wheel of a car. If you notice another vehicle swerving throughout the lane or into other lanes of traffic, this is a common sign that someone might be driving while under the influence. If a person is driving while under the influence of drugs or alcohol, you may see them accelerate or decelerate quickly and at random intervals that you would not see from a sober driver. This may be that they are unable to regulate their speed, or they are not reacting appropriately as they proceed on that route.

While driving under the influence, processing times and reaction times are significantly slower, which means that the driver may take a while before they realize that they are driving too slow or too fast and try to adjust their speed quickly to get to the speed that they should be driving at. Tailgating another driver is another telltale sign that a driver may be under the influence of drugs or alcohol. While under the influence of drugs or alcohol, depth perception is something that suffers, so an impaired driver may not realize that they are as close to the vehicle that is in front of them on the road. It is also common for an individual that is under the influence of drugs or alcohol to follow another vehicle closely to try to stay in the appropriate lanes of traffic.

Regardless of whether or not a driver is under the influence of drugs or alcohol, reckless driving is commonly noticed by seeing the driver doing dangerous traffic maneuvers that put that vehicle and the people around them in danger. Dangerous maneuvers may include swerving in a lane or drifting into another lane. This is a common cause of head on collisions, which are a significant cause of injury or death. Swerving or drifting may happen while the driver is still moving at high speeds, which increases the potential for significant injury or death in the event of an accident.

Tailgating is another dangerous maneuver that you may see from drivers that are experiencing road rage, drivers that are under the influence of drugs or alcohol, or even drivers that are speeding and moving significantly faster than the other vehicles that are around them on that road. Tailgating another vehicle could either lead to that vehicle crashing into the vehicle in front of them because they are speeding, or it could even be an accident because the vehicle in front may have to make a sudden stop and the tailgating vehicle does not have enough room to make the same stop without colliding with the back of the vehicle in front of them.

Reckless driving oftentimes will also be shown through unsafe passing. Unsafe passing is something that you may see in any driving situation and in any location that you may be driving at. Unsafe passing may include passing a school bus that has its lights on and other signals flashing, indicating that it is at a stop to pick up students. If you do pass a school bus that has its indicator lights flashing, not only are you risking a collision with the other vehicles on the road around you, but there is an increased likelihood that you could hit a child that is getting onto the school bus or a parent that has walked their child to the school bus stop.

On smaller back roads and country roads, unsafe passing of another vehicle could mean passing them at a speed significantly higher than is safe if the road has a steep hill or sharp turn. If you pass a vehicle with a steep hill in front of you, you cannot get a clear view of any other vehicles that may be approaching you from the opposite direction. If you pass leading up to a sharp turn, not only are you also risking a collision with a vehicle that you cannot see, but moving at high speeds around a sharp turn could result in the vehicle rolling over. These roads are also commonly surrounded by various wildlife, and if you pass another vehicle, this could lead to you not seeing an animal on the side of the road or crossing the road, leading to a collision that could cause significant injury, along with significant damage to your vehicle.

No matter what type of roadway that you are driving on, the lines in the road are universal for telling you whether you can pass in an area or if passing in that area should not happen. On a road with multiple lanes moving in the same direction, there will be an individual line dividing each of the lanes. If the color of the dividing line is white, that means that the vehicles in those lanes are moving in the same direction. If the single lane that is dividing traffic is a dashed line, that means that passing is permitted in that area.

If a roadway does have two lines dividing the lanes of the road, they will typically be yellow, indicating that the traffic on that road is going in opposite directions. If the lines that are dividing those lanes of traffic are both solid lines, that means that there is no passing that is permitted in that area on either side of the road. If one side of the road is a solid line while the other is a dashed line, only the traffic that is on the side of the road with the dashed line is permitted to pass vehicles. If you are on a road like this, it is crucial to make sure that you are looking ahead to ensure that the roadway is clear of any other traffic that is coming from the opposite direction. Before passing in this situation, make sure that you are checking multiple times before proceeding to make the pass. You should also never pass on a roadway like this if you are coming to the end of the dashed line. When passing on a roadway with a dashed line, both at the beginning of your passing and the end of the passing maneuver should happen when the line is still dashed. You should never begin or end your passing maneuver in a location where the lines in the road have returned to being a solid line.

For smaller highways, such as highways in rural areas that are one lane in each direction, there are times where you may see other drivers passing a turning vehicle on the right shoulder. This is extremely dangerous and is something that you should never do under any circumstance. If you pass another vehicle on the shoulder, not only are you risking an accident if the vehicle makes a sudden decision to move forward instead of making the turn, but you are also risking getting into an accident with a vehicle that is turning in the opposite direction that may not see you if you are passing on the shoulder.

As technology continues to evolve, distracted driving continues to increase its roll in reckless driving incidents. Whether you are looking at a GPS or phone maps application for directions, reading a text message, or streaming a show from your favorite channel, distracted driving takes your focus away from the road, which can lead to any of the reckless behaviors that have been described up until this point. Distracted driving is not only looking at your phone or any other device, but distracted driving could also be someone putting on makeup while driving down the road, or a busy parent handling their children while fighting in the back seat.

If you are driving recklessly, whether it is intentional or unintentional, the consequences for your actions can be severe. If you are speeding and surpass the threshold of 15 or 20 miles per hour over the speed limit as deemed by the state that you are driving in, not only will you be facing a speeding ticket, but you will also be cited for reckless driving. This may be a fine in some states, but in others it is a misdemeanor that would require you to go to court. If you do need to go to court because of a reckless driving charge, not only are you looking at paying for the fines of driving recklessly, but there are also court fees and paying a lawyer that may be required, depending on the circumstances.

Not only can reckless driving be costly to you financially in court if you are pulled over, but if you get into an accident while driving recklessly, you are facing the financial hardship of the damage to your vehicle, the damage to the other vehicle if there was a collision with another vehicle, but also any property damage that may occur, such as hitting a guard rail or driving into a field. Reckless driving also puts you, your passengers, and everyone around you at risk of significant injury or even death.

Driving recklessly can also lead to you being arrested, your driver's license being either suspended or revoked, points added to your driver's license, or the vehicle that you were driving recklessly being impounded. All of these not only have significant financial repercussions but could also have a significant impact on the other parts of your life, such as in your home life or even with your ability to work.

STAYING SAFE AROUND A RECKLESS DRIVER

When you are driving, you may be around a reckless driver, and there are a few things that you can do to make sure that you are staying safe in those situations. When getting behind the wheel of a car, it is important to make sure that you leave where you are starting your route with plenty of time to get to your destination. If you are running late, not only can this lead to additional unnecessary stress and road rage situations, but it can also lead to speeding and other dangerous maneuvers that are reckless, and end up putting yourself, your passengers, and the other people on the road at risk.

Along with making sure to relieve some of the stressors that may cause reckless driving, it is important to maintain a safe following distance, especially if you notice that another driver around you is driving in a reckless manner. If you follow the reckless driver too closely, this could put you at risk of an accident if that driver swerves suddenly or even makes a sudden stop. Ensuring that you have enough distance between your vehicle and the other vehicles or obstacles that are around you makes sure that you have time to react if another driver does make a sudden move that is dangerous.

While you are driving, staying focused on the road, and the other vehicles that are on the road is an important way to make sure that you are staying safe and keeping your passengers safe as well. If you are driving while distracted, not only are you driving recklessly and putting the people around you at risk, but you are also going to be unable to see anyone else who may be driving recklessly.

Making sure that you are staying safe while driving down the road is one of the best ways that you will be able to protect yourself from other drivers who are driving in a reckless manner. Make sure that while you are driving, you are following the laws of the road where you are driving, including obeying speed limits, stop signs and traffic lights.

BECOMING THE BEST DRIVER YOU CAN

You have finally made it to the end of this important guide of everything that you need to know as a new driver. Throughout this journey, you have learned about the process of getting your learner's permit and eventually your driver's license, how to practice driving, what to do if you get into an accident or your vehicle breaks down, and so much more.

Keep in mind that as you go out into the world as a brand new driver and this is just the beginning. There are a lot of things that you will need to know as a driver, both as a beginner just learning and even ten years down the road if any traffic laws are changed, added, or even removed. Being the best driver that you can be involves constantly studying to make sure that you know what is happening on the roads, and following all traffic laws while you are out on the road.

Being the best driver that you can be starts with making sure that you are prepared for what you will encounter on the road in real life situations, and this book is the first step, but it is also making sure that you are staying focused on the road and following every law. Regardless of your own personal opinions, the rules of the road have been created to keep you, any passengers in your vehicle, and the other drivers and pedestrians on the road stay as safe as possible. Do not pick and choose which of the rules of the road that you are going to follow, make sure that you understand and that you are following all of them all the time.

Driving is a significant responsibility that you should never take lightly. While it is important to be able to drive to get to another location, such as school or work, driving is a privilege and not a right. At any point, if you are driving in an unsafe manner or cause an accident, your ability to drive can be taken away. Not only does driving safe make sure that you are able to continue driving as needed, but it also makes sure that you do not get into an accident that takes away your physical ability to drive through injury or even death.

The people around you, those who love you, cannot replace you. If you do not drive in a safe way, you are risking the possibility of death, not only ending your life, but permanently changing the lives of the people who care about you. Even if you do not do it for yourself, keep those that are close to you in mind every time you get behind the wheel of the car. It could be the thing that makes you think twice, drive a little safer, and could even be the thing to save your life.

If you are taking a trip, whether it is alone or with others, there are things that you need to do to make sure that everyone stays safe before hitting the road. The pre-driving check of the vehicle will help to make sure that you are aware of any issues with the vehicle that may need to be addressed so that you can avoid a breakdown or accident. When getting into the vehicle, before you even turn the car on, make sure that every person that is riding in that vehicle is wearing their seat belt properly. Wearing a seat belt is one small thing that could be the difference between life and death.

Along with staying vigilant about safety while you are driving, the more that you drive, the more confident you will become with your driving abilities. As you spend more time driving, practice is something that you can always do to be as confident as you can in your abilities behind the wheel. Practice parallel parking or merging onto a larger road. The only way that you are going to be a confident driver is through practicing those skills until you have mastered them. While each state may have their minimum requirements that you must meet before you are able to get your driver's license, that does not mean that you are done learning and done practicing your driving skills. It will take several years before you are truly the most confident driver that you can be and that is only going to happen through time, patience, and most importantly, practice!

Printed in Great Britain
by Amazon